Glimpses of God's Heart

Divinely Inspired Daily Devotions

Gwen Wellington

Endorsements

"God is desperately in love with us! Gwen's recording of God's love song for her challenges readers to question whether humanity has ever been separate from the Divine.

Many people have an intellectual "knowing" of God through reading sacred texts, but Gwen has shared her experiential "knowing" of God through prayer.

Intimacy with God can be felt within the context of deep pain. Gwen has tapped into the cosmic truth that God weeps with us when we are feeling alone, alienated and without meaning.

Because humans are much more than just intellect, the presence of the Divine can be felt in other ways that go beyond printed words. Reading *Glimpses of God's Heart*, leaves the reader with a felt sense of God's deep participation in our humanity."

~ Dr. Cheryl A. Noble, Psychologist

"Truly, this grand devotional book is a matter of the heart. Gwen has opened to us all her most private times in that Secret Place with the Lord. As I read the writings in this book, tears filled my eyes at times, as I saw the love that our Lord has for us and how this God, the Creator of the universe, is open to communicate with us in such an intimate way.

These devotional readings will inspire you to develop an intimacy with the Lord. They will encourage you to journal your times with the Lord, found in that Secret Place.

My hope is that, after you have read this book daily, you will say of the Lord, "I have heard of You by the hearing of the ear, but now my eyes see You." (Job 42:5)"

~ Dr. Hazel Hill, co-founder of Victory Churches International and best-selling author of *Praying God's Word*.

For more inspiration and motivation, visit Gwen's blog at
www.wellington-author.com/blog/.

Glimpses of God's Heart
Divinely Inspired Daily Devotions
Copyright © 2017 by Gwen Wellington

ISBN-10: 1981461736
ISBN-13: 978-1981461738

Dedication

To my mother

who led me to invite Jesus into my life
when I was a little girl

and

to my father

whose gentle, affectionate, and fun-loving manner
invited me to think that God might be like that.

Foreword

In this set of devotions, Gwen invites us into her love affair with God. She paints a portrait of God—intimate, loving, compassionate, endlessly pursuing us so that we might turn into God's tender embrace. These are the words and reflections of a faithful woman. Throughout her life, Gwen has learned to rest within the embrace of a God who loves and accepts us as we are, and at the same time loves us too much to leave us the way we are.

These are words spoken between two lovers. They are intimate words. They bespeak a deep love and a longing for closeness and affection. These words are whispered in the light and in the darkest recesses of the soul. They are words of joy and sorrow, hope and despair. These words are born in the interplay between wonder and apprehension. These words live in seasons marked by sunshine and dark clouds.

Gwen paints images of God in a wide variety of hues and colors. She has an incalculable imagination as she seeks to splash her vision of God on the canvas of these pages. She uses playful images that delight in the love that pours from God's heart for all of God's creation. Her images are powerful as they draw us into a more intimate relationship with God, and make our hearts dare to believe more deeply that God's love is surely for us all.

Finally, Gwen has been in labor with this book throughout her adult life. The final push towards birth came with the medical crisis of her subdural hematoma. An urgency was born in her soul to give birth to this book. Each day now has an intense pleasure, the colors of the world more vibrant, the thrumming of God's heart within her more vigorous.

In these words, I hear echoes of some of the great mystics of the past—Teresa of Avila, Julian of Norwich, Hildegard of Bingen. Gwen's words of pleasure and passion give us a glimpse into the heart of God, and are filled with hope and love.

In Book 8, Chapter 12 of his *Confessions*, St. Augustine tells of hearing a young child chanting, "Take up and read." It was a conversion moment for him. I encourage you to take up and read. You will find your own heart touched deeply by these glimpses into God's heart.

~ Rev. Dr. Yme Woensdregt
Christ Church Anglican
Cranbrook, BC

Introduction

I am delighted that you found your way to this book! With each of these devotional readings, I am inviting you to join God and me in that sacred space where we share our hearts with each other. You can expect to be encouraged, comforted, delighted, challenged, inspired or maybe even surprised as you read the entry for each day.

Let me tell you how this book came to be.

Journaling is a life coping technique that I have practiced for much of my adult life. Most of my journaling has consisted of writing down the conversations I have with God. This book is the fruit of a decision that I made in 1979 to write down not only what I am saying to God, but also what I sense God is saying to me. *Glimpses of God's Heart* is a selection of 366 of the many hundreds of things I have sensed God saying to me during the past thirty-eight years.

When I began writing these words, I had no idea that they would one distant day find their way into a book. What happened, however, is that as I shared the readings with friends and family members from time to time, I began receiving encouragement to publish them. The final push that catapulted me into the work of compiling the readings in this book came a year and a half ago, when a dear friend was so blessed by one that she said, "Gwen, you have to get those readings out and now!" And so, that is how my private conversations with God have now become public knowledge. No one is more surprised than I!

Let me say a little bit about how these "words" from God come to me. I do not hear an audible voice. I do not experience automatic writing that involves setting aside the conscious mind. I do not see visions. Instead, I quiet my soul – my mind, my will, and my emotions – and then I sense concepts or feelings from God in my spirit, or the core of my being. I write down what I am sensing, rephrasing it until what I have written accurately reflects what I am sensing.

This business of quieting my soul is no small task, involving as it does silencing the chatter in my mind, letting go of whatever I might want, and weaning my emotions. To my surprise and frustration, this task has not gotten easier over the years. As you will find out, I am a very ordinary person who experiences all the typical vicissitudes and frailties of human life!

You might be wondering how I can know that what I sense comes from God. This is a reasonable question to ask, and you can be sure that I have asked it as well! One way, perhaps the main way, to test the source of the thoughts or ideas I sense is to check them against the Bible, the Judeo-Christian scriptures. When I was a young adult, I spent four years studying the Bible at a Bible College.[1] Over the years, I have continued to immerse myself in these scriptures by meditating on them and memorizing them. This familiarity with the Bible, commonly referred to as "God's Word," helps me to know whether or not what I am sensing originates with God.

I invite you to participate in this testing process. I have included many footnotes that are references to places in scripture that reflect the ideas in the text. Sometimes I have indicated a

---

[1] Canadian Mennonite Bible College, now Canadian Mennonite University, in Winnipeg, Manitoba.

specific translation that suits best. I would like to recommend a web site that makes it really easy to find scriptures, and to read them in 25 different translations: biblehub.com.   Click on "Parallel" (for parallel translations) and type in the scripture reference in the search bar at the top.

Reading this book will never replace the benefit of reading the Bible. The words in these devotionals do not take the place of, or add to, the revelation of a loving and merciful God that we find in scriptures. One of my reasons for including footnotes that are references to scriptures, is to direct you to that original and authentic word of the God who I have found to be the true source of life.

Over the many years of listening, I have discovered that God uses what I have experienced in life to speak to me. Because I worked as a psychotherapist for twenty-four years, not infrequently God speaks to me in the language of that field. The benefit of that for you is that some of the readings contain the kind of wisdom you would receive if you were sitting in the office of a psychosocial counselor. Of course, reading this book in no way will replace the benefit you can gain from hiring a good counselor when you find yourself unable to work through something on your own.

If you have experience with the Twelve Step program for addicts and co-addicts, you will recognize familiar themes such as shame, letting go, and craving approval. This is because I struggle with codependence. It would be true to say that the devotionals in this book provide an intimate view of my efforts to do Step Three: handing my will and my life over to the care of God as I understand God. I offer them to you in the hope that my sharing will encourage you on your recovery journey.

Let me give you two examples of how these readings are created in my life.

Four years ago, I found myself in the disconcerting situation of wrapping up my counseling practice without any clear sense of where I was headed. All I knew was that my body was telling me I had to make a change. I felt lost and very sad, because I loved my counseling work and I couldn't conceive that anything else would ever be as rewarding and satisfying. The following words from God became my anchor as I navigated the transition.

My treasure, my love:
Even though you feel lost, you're not.
Even though you think you don't know the way, you do.
Even though you think you're giving up
something extremely valuable,
You simply are making room
for something just as valuable.
Walk confidently into the future, my love!
I have such joy planned for you!
Embrace this time of change and the change itself.
Know that I surround you and I go before you.
I fill you and I energize you.
It's you and me together,
sashaying boldly into the future.
You'll see!
What joy!
Pure, unadulterated joy!
You and me together.
Yes. I like it!!

More recently, I experienced lying on a hospital bed while waiting for burr hole surgery to relieve the pressure on my brain created by a subdural hematoma (brain bleed). I was in excruciating pain and losing the ability to function physically and to think or to even know where I was. The one thought I do remember having as I neared death was, "I'm being reduced to nothing." All I could do was to cry out to God, "Jesus, save me!" over and over again. The surgery brought blissful relief. Several days later, these words from God helped me to come to terms with this traumatic event:

My treasure:
I have been closer than your heartbeat
through this entire experience.
I surely carried you
when you were too weak
to even know where you were.
This water of adversity has not swept you away,
but rather is being used to do a sorting and a sifting
that will bring positive change.
The truth is that nothing can separate you from my love,
not physical pain or disorientation
or loss of physical or mental or emotional function.
When you cried out to me for help,
that cry was the breath of my Spirit within you,
interceding for you with groans too deep for words.
I am answering those prayers, my love!

In this way, each of the devotional readings in this book has been birthed as I walk through my life experiences together with God.

My hope is that the glimpses of God's heart revealed in these readings will speak to you in a life-giving way, and that my sharing with you my experience of intimacy with God will encourage you to cultivate and enjoy that place for yourself.

January

January 1

My love, my treasure:
Look no further than within to find your source,
for I am pleased to make my home there.[1]
Yes, I am very pleased to rest within you.
I'm relaxing here within you –
I've found a comfy spot
and I'm waiting to chat with you any time.
We can talk about anything you like.
Take that decision you are trying to make, for example.
Let's talk about that.
You are vacillating. Unsure.
You can know if you are going in the flow of my Spirit
because this is accompanied by peace and enthusiasm
even if the endeavor is challenging or even scary.
Going against the flow of my Spirit
is characterized by resistance and heaviness.
Remember:
Even if you make a decision that seems wrong in retrospect,
I can and will use that decision for good.[2]
So relax, my love, and go with the flow!

---

[1] John 14:23; John 17:23; 1 Corinthians 3:16; Revelation 3:20.
[2] Romans 8:28.

January 2

My treasure:
I want you to know, for once and for all,
that my approval does not rest on your performance.[1]
I approve of you because of who you are.[2]
What you do or do not do has no bearing on my approval.
I love you for who are.
You do not need to do anything.
You don't even need to love me in return.
I still will love you.
I still will dote on you.
I still will treasure you.[3]
This is the attitude you are to have towards yourself: unconditional
love and approval for who you are.
Behavior is secondary.
You know this is true because you experience it
in your relationship with your children:
You love them unconditionally;
no matter what they do or don't do,
you love them fully.
Love yourself the same way.
Some behavior may need to be changed,
but who you are is completely acceptable.
I created you and declared my creation to be good.[4]
Very good, my love!

---

[1] Titus 3:4-5; Ephesians 2:4-5.
[2] 1 John 3:1.
[3] Luke 15:11-32.
[4] Genesis 1:31.

January 3

Precious child:
I see that smile on your face –
it's mirroring the smile on my face!
I love this place of gratitude you have found,
and I love your determination to stay there.
Today I want to remind you
that there is no condemnation for you
because I have placed you in Christ Jesus.[1]
Let go of all guilt-inducing thoughts.
There simply is no condemnation for you!
Your sins are always forgiven – past, present, and future.[2]
You are totally free from guilt and shame
because I achieved that for you.
This is my gift of salvation.[3]
You know when you have missed the mark in your behavior
because this is accompanied by a sense of uneasiness.
Simply begin again with no need for any condemnation.
Condemnation accomplishes nothing good!
My heart is bursting with joy and pride
when I consider you, my love![4]
I'm so looking forward to spending this year with you!

---

[1] Romans 8:1.
[2] Colossians 1:13-14; Acts 13:38; Ephesians 1:7.
[3] Ephesians 2:8.
[4] Psalm 147:11; Psalm 149:4; Zephaniah 3:17.

January 4

Precious treasure:
The Elijah story[1] is the story
of someone who experienced excruciating despair
because he had incomplete information.
He was extrapolating
from only a few pieces of the picture puzzle.
What he could see was bad –
yes, it truly was bad –
but I was not finished working out my purposes.[2]
On the basis of what Elijah could see,
it was understandable that he felt so terrible
that he wanted to die.
Anyone would have wanted to.
Even that great hero of the faith!
And so it is with you.
On the basis of what you can see,
it is understandable that you feel so terrible
that you want to die.
What I have to say to you, however,
is that I have not yet finished working out my purpose.
The only way out of this despair
that holds you in a death grip
is to surrender this circumstance into my loving care.[3]
And when you have done so,
you will be free to live and even to rejoice
whilst you cannot yet see what is going on.

---

[1] 1 Kings 18-19.
[2] Ephesians 1:11; Isaiah 46:10.
[3] 1 Peter 5:7.

January 5

My treasure, my love:
I am the God of limitless creativity.
I am the God of endless solutions and possibilities.[1]
My treasure, my love:
Tap into this wellspring
and let it flow in the unique way that is yours.
Yours.
And only yours.
Just do it.
Let go of all doubt.
Throw caution to the wind.
And proceed.
With joy.
You have my blessing and my life to draw on.[2]

---

[1] Mark 10:27; Jeremiah 32:17.
[2] 2 Corinthians 9:8; Ephesians 3:20; Philippians 4:19; 1 Corinthians 3:16.

January 6

My treasure:
You are wondering about my presence
within creation and within you.
Let me talk to you about this.
I am greater than anything in creation,
including any power or force or energy.[1]
These are all things that I created[2]
and that I use to build my Kingdom on earth –
my Kingdom of righteousness, peace, and joy.[3]
The closest you can come to experiencing me
is in the area of love.[4]
Wherever you see love expressed, you see me.
Anything done with the motivation of love[5]
is close to my heart.
Love captures the essence of the life of Jesus.
It was his love for me and for creation that motivated him.
The only pure motivation is love.[6]
Because I am love, my love is primarily what you sense
when you become aware of my presence within you.[7]
Your new life in Christ[8] is my life of love
reaching out to love the world.

---

[1] Psalm 113:4; John 3:31; Ephesians 1:18-22.
[2] Colossians 1:16.
[3] Romans 14:17.
[4] 1 John 4:16.
[5] 1 Corinthians 16:14.
[6] 1 Corinthians 13.
[7] 1 John 4:16.
[8] Romans 6:4; 2 Corinthians 5:17; Colossians 2:12; Colossians 3:1; 1 Peter 1:3.

January 7

Treasure:
I am within you,
helping you to figure out
whether or not to take advantage of this opportunity.[1]
There is no need to be concerned.
It all will become clear in time.
Be guided by this question, "What will give me joy?"[2]
If it doesn't give you joy, simply don't do it.
In fact, do everything with joy.[3]
This is how you practice having my joy
and how you experience being strengthened by my joy.

---

[1] Philippians 2:13.
[2] Psalm 16:11.
[3] Deuteronomy 12:7.

January 8

My treasure, my love:
Get your hopes up.
This is one of those things that look bad but lead to good.
This is one of those areas where I am working for your good.[1]
It also is related to my Kingdom being built.
So don't despair.
Keep hoping.
Keep believing.
Keep trusting in my goodness and my love.[2]

---

[1] Romans 8:28.
[2] Psalm 109:21; Titus 3:3-8; 1 John 4:7-12.

January 9

Death is just as K*ü*bler-Ross[1] describes it – transition from this world, from this bodily state, to the next world. Death merely marks a change in the way you and I relate: Now you know me imperfectly; then you shall know me as I am.[2] Death is the time when you part with all that you perceive through your bodily senses and enter fully into the realm that you perceive by the spirit. It is the transition from life in the flesh to life in the spirit.

Death is not to be feared.[3] Life itself does not end. Although life as you know it ends, a new life begins. The deceiver will try to make you fearful by presenting false accusations and lies.[4] Resist this.[5] I am with you always and will guide you safely through this transition.

To understand death, it is helpful see your life from my perspective. I am the Lord. From the foundations of the earth, I planned for you.[6] When the time was right, I created a body for you and breathed into you the breath of life.[7] When the time is right, I will set your spirit free of its earthly body to join me in my heavenly position and state.[8]

---

[1] Elisabeth K*ü*bler-Ross was a Swiss psychiatrist who wrote a book, *On Death and Dying* (New York: The Macmillan Company, 1969), based on her work with terminally ill patients and their loved ones.
[2] 1 Corinthians 13:12.
[3] Hebrews 2:14-15.
[4] John 8:44.
[5] James 4:7.
[6] Psalm 138:8 (New Living Translation – NLT); Psalm 139; Ephesians 1:4.
[7] Genesis 2:7.
[8] Luke 23:43; Jude 1:21.

January 10

My dear child:
Your faith is like a seed that you plant and unearth,
plant again and unearth.
It will never thrive and grow strong if you keep doing this.
Plant it and leave it.
Water it with my Word.
Warm it with positive confession.
Chase away the darkness of doubt.
There is time even now for you to invest a tiny bit of faith
and realize a huge profit in trust and confidence.
Plant the seed of faith that I will respond to your request
and never question it again,
regardless of the circumstances.[1]

---

[1] Mark 11:24; James 1:6.

January 11

My treasure, my love:
Your life is about a love relationship with me.[1]
It's about learning that you live in my love
and that you are safe there in all circumstances,
whether prison or bankruptcy
or famine or getting sued
or getting cancer
or your child dying
or anything.
You are safe there, even if you make mistakes.
So no matter what happens, you live in my love.[2]
This was Jesus' prayer: "I in them and you in me."[3]
My love is in you, permeating you, enveloping you.
So relax.
Let it be.
Let this knowledge bring healing to your joints,[4]
my precious, my darling.

---

[1] 1 John 4:16; Revelation 3:20; John 14:23.
[2] Romans 8:38-39.
[3] John 17:23a (New International Version – NIV).
[4] Proverbs 3:7-8; Proverb 4:20-22; Isaiah 66:13-14a.

January 12

My love, my treasure;
I see your exhaustion.
I know your limitations.
More than anyone, I know your limitations.
Please choose to trust me.[1]
Trust that I am looking after everything.
You will look back on this time and marvel at my provision.
Choose to trust me.
Choose to trust my loving care.
Choose to believe that I am in charge.
Choose to believe that I am providing for you with generosity –
With extravagant generosity, actually.[2]
I love you, my treasure.
I love you, my precious child.
Choose to lean on my tender loving care.

---

[1] Isaiah 26:4; Proverbs 3:5.
[2] 1 Timothy 6:17.

January 13

My words for you today, dear friend,
concern your life of submission.[1]
As you submit to me, I submit to you.
I, God Almighty, submit to you, my created vessel,
for this is the way of power and plenty and peace and love.
Do not think of submission as an act of weakness.
No.
It takes great courage and strength to submit.
It takes long-suffering and wisdom to submit.
Meditate on my submission[2]
and you will see the sublime beauty and overcoming strength
of this action and attitude.
I love to submit because I love.
To love is to give and to give is to submit –
to yield one's life and resources to another.
This is a holy way and a way of victory.
Always take advantage of every opportunity to submit.
It is my way and I have set the example for you.
As I submit to you, so I ask you to submit to others.[3]
Pour out your life for others
and you will find my life rising up within you.

---

[1] James 4:7a.
[2] Philippians 2:5-11; John 13:3-5.
[3] Ephesians 5:21.

January 14

Dear friend, I am here, surrounding you and filling you.[1]

Fasting is something I ask of all my followers.[2] It proves to them, first of all, that the body is subject to the spirit: You are in control of your body. This is a great help in curbing the lusts of the flesh, for in fasting you learn to deny the flesh. You can say, "No, I do not need this." "I can do without this." "I can wait for this." "I will not let my body tell me what to do." And so on.

What you can say to your body, you can also say to your mind and emotions. In this way your spirit takes its rightful place as master. Because your spirit is united with mine, you become Spirit-directed and your life bears fruit.[3]

Fasting, secondly, proves to you and to the spirit world that you are serious about your intention. You are prepared to deny yourself to get what you want. What you take seriously, I take seriously.

Thirdly, fasting sets in motion battles in the heavenlies.[4] You are cooperating very directly with crushing the head of the serpent.[5] In time you will see this.

---

[1] Ephesians 5:18b.
[2] Matthew 6:16-18.
[3] John 15:1-17.
[4] See Daniel 10 for an account of fasting and ensuing battles in the heavenlies (spiritual territories). Ephesians 6:12.
[5] Romans 16:20; Luke 10:19.

January 15

Let me speak words of love to you, my precious treasure!
I love being united with you!
I am always at work, perfecting our unity,
because I love you and I love living within you!
I created you as a dwelling place for me
and it gives me great pleasure to be in you.[1]
Dear friend, I long to share my life with you:
my thoughts, my feelings, my desires, and my endeavors.[2]
Never doubt this!
I cherish every second you spend communing with me.

---

[1] Revelation 3:20; John 14:23.
[2] Jeremiah 33:3.

January 16

Unbelief is the greatest sin.[1]
It is the root of all sin.
It paves the way for all other sin to flourish.
Love always trusts, always believes.[2]
Choose always to believe
and you will prosper in unimaginable ways,[3]
for faith is the key to abundant life.[4]
Curse unbelief!
Develop a hatred for it that parallels mine!
You have treated it as a minor annoyance
instead of the loathsome evil that it is.

---

[1] Matthew 13:58; Hebrews 3:12; Hebrews 3:18-19.
[2] 1 Corinthians 13:7.
[3] 2 Chronicles 20:20.
[4] Hebrews 11:6.

January 17

My love, my treasure:
Open your heart and listen
to my still, small voice
speak tenderly to you.[1]
I am not upset with you.
I am not displeased with you.
I am not disappointed with you.
I am not shaking my head in despair.
Nor am I shaking my finger in admonishment.
No!
Instead, I am smiling, my love.
I am smiling with pleasure because I delight in you.[2]
Receive the warmth of my smile.

---

[1] 1 Kings 19:11-13 (NLT).
[2] Zephaniah 3:17 (NLT); Mark 1:11.

January 18

My love, my treasure:
I love you.
Find your home, your place to belong, in me.[1]
Move in. Set up housekeeping.
Make it permanent. Hang pictures.
Don't just rent – buy. Own.[2]
Sell your soul for this place
of comfort sweet[3]
near to the heart of God.
In the heart of God![4]

---

[1] Romans 1:6; Colossians 3:3; Acts 17:28.
[2] Matthew 13:44.
[3] 2 Corinthians 1:3-4.
[4] Colossians 3:3.

January 19

My treasure, quiet your soul [1]and listen.

Do not be surprised at this trial, as though it was something unexpected and uncalled for.[2] In this world you **will** have trials and temptations. Do not, however, be dismayed, for I have overcome the world and I live within you.[3] Yield to me. Allow me to use these trials to cleanse you. Do not resist the work of my Holy Spirit.

You are the apple of my eye.[4] Remember that nothing can separate you from my love,[5] and nothing can thwart my plan for your life except your willful disobedience.[6] So do not be discouraged. I am at work in you, causing you to will and to do my purpose,[7] and the gates of hell[8] are not able to stop my advancing the Kingdom through you. Never forget that I have chosen you[9] and I will be faithful to complete the work that I have begun in and through you.[10]

So rest in me. I am the Prince of Peace.[11] I fight the battles and you claim the victories. List all your battles and know that I am fighting them for you.[12] Remain yielded and humble before me, and enter my rest.[13] Rest, my little one - for I am your strong and mighty Lord.

---

[1] Psalm 131:2; Psalm 62:1.
[2] 1 Peter 4:12.
[3] John 16:33.
[4] Psalm 17:8; Proverbs 7:2; Deuteronomy 32:10.
[5] Romans 8:38-39.
[6] Psalm 138:8 (NLT); Psalm 32:8-9.
[7] Philippians 2:13.
[8] Matthew 16:18.
[9] 1 Peter 2:9.
[10] Philippians 1:6.
[11] Isaiah 9:6.
[12] 1 Samuel 17:47.
[13] Matthew 11:28-29.

January 20

My treasure, my love:
If you knew what I know, if you could see what I see,
you would not worry about anything, you would not be anxious,
and you would not get defensive and lash out in anger.
I am in control, my treasure.
I am not distant, nor capricious, nor uncaring.
I am leading and guiding you every step of the way.[1]
At a later time you will look back
and stand amazed at what I have done.
Take courage from stories in the bible –
stories relating my leading and guiding and providing.
Know that I am the same yesterday, today, and forever.[2]
I know your heart's cry – be assured that I am on it!
Each day, as you pray, I send angels to do my Word.[3]
Do not let anything come between us –
not your sins or even your mistakes.
Know that I am a good God.
Know also that I delight in you,
for you sincerely reach out to me in faith.
It is faith that pleases me.[4]
So relax and enjoy every aspect of your life.
Reach out to me with child-like trust and abandonment.
I will not let you down.
There may be times when you do not understand (or like!)
my ways or my timing,
but know that it is always in your best interests.
Dear child – I want you to be happy, to be carefree, to be joyful,[5]
and to be intimate with me.
Lift up your head and be glad!

---

[1] Psalm 32:8 (NLT).
[2] Hebrews 13:8.
[3] Matthew 26:53.
[4] Hebrews 11:6.
[5] 1 Thessalonians 5:16; Philippians 4:4.

January 21

Let's have a chat, my love, about prayers that appear to remain unanswered.

First, I want to tell you that I have loved every one of your prayers.

Any prayer is prayed with faith and it is faith that pleases me.[1]

Secondly, your prayers come from your heart's desire and your best understanding of situations. As such, they are perfect.

Thirdly, I take all your prayers and use them to build my Kingdom. It is not necessary for you to understand this – just trust that I am doing it.

Having said this, there are some helpful attitudes that you can take while approaching and engaging in prayer.

In the first place, prayer is best approached with an attitude of humility.[2] Know that you are human: your understanding is limited, you will make mistakes, and you do not always know what is best.

A second attitude that is helpful is to approach prayer with a grateful heart.[3] Be thankful for the opportunity to pray and for the opportunity to work together with me to build my Kingdom through prayer.

Thirdly, approaching prayer with an attitude of hope and expectancy brings freedom to pray.[4]

---

[1] Hebrews 11:6.
[2] James 4:10.
[3] Philippians 4:6.
[4] Romans 12:12.

January 22

In my treasure pouch, I have many precious jewels.[1]
You are one of them.
I hold you in my hand
and enjoy the sparkle of the radiance of my Son
reflected in your beauty.[2]
You bring me great joy, my child![3]
Every day, as I cradle you in my hands,
I continue to cleanse and polish you.[4]
Sometimes the cleansing goes deep into a shaft or crevice –
perhaps to the core of your being.
As you work with me,
expressing your anger
and crying your tears of grief
and speaking words of forgiveness,
you are healed.
My love,
expressed in the blood of the Lamb[5],
brings healing.

---

[1] 1 Samuel 25:29 (NLT).
[2] 2 Corinthians 3:18.
[3] Zephaniah 3:17; Psalm 147:11 (NLT); Psalm 149:4.
[4] Psalm 19:12 (NLT); Psalm 51.
[5] 1 Peter 1:18-19.

January 23

Lovely one:
You are my treasure.[1]
I delight in you.
I rejoice over you with songs of love.[2]
I encourage you to look deep into your spirit
and see my face reflected there.
Even the desires in your innermost being reflect my desires.
Do not think there is ever a second
when you and I are not in communion![3]
I am closer to you than you can imagine.

---

[1] Exodus 19:5 (NLT); Malachi 3:17 (NLT); Revelation 3:20.
[2] Zephaniah 3:17.
[3] 1 Corinthians 3:16; 1 Corinthians 6:19; John 14:23.

January 24

My treasure, my child:
Look to me and live.[1]
Look to me and live.
Yes! Look to me and live –
for I am your all in all.
In me, you lack nothing.[2]
"…I know the plans I have for you…
plans to prosper you and not to harm you,
plans to give you hope and a future."[3]
My treasure, my lovely:
Know that you are a smile on my face and joy in my heart.[4]
You and I –
we are not nearly finished working together in my Kingdom.
You and I are partners in a work that is only just beginning.[5]
Continue to allow me to heal you and set you free
to fully participate in this effort.
You are my chosen instrument.[6]
I am carefully shaping you
and establishing you in this endeavor.
It will bring you great joy – a joy you already taste.
My treasure, my love:
You are the smile on my face, the joy in my heart.
There is no fear in this place you have in my being.[7]
Dwell in me and I will dwell in you.[8]

---

[1] Isaiah 45:22.
[2] Psalm 23:1; Psalm 34:10.
[3] Jeremiah 29:11 (NIV).
[4] Zephaniah 3:17.
[5] 1 Corinthians 1:9 (NLT); 1 Corinthians 3:9; 2 Corinthians 6:1.
[6] John 15:16; 1 Peter 2:9.
[7] 1 John 4:18.
[8] John 15:4.

January 25

My love, my treasure:
I am talking to you all the time![1]
I am speaking in your thoughts,
your emotions,
and your motivations.
I speak through your desires,
through conviction,
and through my Word.
I speak through books and movies and billboards....
I am not silent.
The earth shouts my voice![2]
I am not silent.
But you must be silent to hear.
You must pay attention to hear.
My treasure, my love:
I am better than a friend because I am with you always.[3]
"Be still, and know that I am God"[4]
and I am speaking to you.
And, by the way, I also speak through circumstances.

---

[1] Psalm 29.
[2] Isaiah 44:23.
[3] Matthew 28:20b.
[4] Psalm 46:10a (English Standard Version – ESV).

January 26

Stop worrying about whether or not you get answers –
just pray![1]
Leave the results in my hands.
Ask me for what you want and I will give it to you.[2]
Some answers take years, even decades or centuries to create,[3] so
submit your requests and let them go.
With thanksgiving.[4]
Trust my Spirit within you to motivate you to pray my will
and I will bring these things to pass.[5]
In my time.

---

[1] 1 Thessalonians 5:17.
[2] Matthew 7:7; 1 John 3:22.
[3] Hebrews 11:13.
[4] Philippians 4:6,
[5] Philippians 2:13.

January 27

My lovely, my treasure:
I am your Source, your Life.
Celebrate my life within you.[1]
Know that I have every day of your life planned
with infinite possibilities for you to do my will.[2]
My treasure, my lovely:
Relax and live.
You need fear nothing nor be anxious about anything.[3]
I am your God.[4]
Meditate on my Word and be fed daily.
And mostly: enjoy my life within you,
motivating you, healing you, equipping you…
I delight in you!
I "rejoice over you with singing."[5]
So relax and enjoy your life to the best of your ability.

[1] Job 33:4; Galatians 2:20.
[2] Psalm 139:16.
[3] Isaiah 41:10; Matthew 6:25-34.
[4] Isaiah 41:10, 13; Ezekiel 34:31.
[5] Zephaniah 3:17 (NIV).

January 28

My treasure, my love:
"Be still, and know that I am God."[1]
"Be still, and know that I am (**your**) God."[2]
I may be Lord of all, but I am also **your** God.
I care about you.[3]
I care about every detail in your life.[4]
I have a vested interest in you.
Don't be duped or misled: I am looking after every detail.
I am looking after details that you have no notion exist.
Your life is in my hands.[5]
So go forth with joy and carefree abandon.
You have a destiny that I created in your genes:
Live it.
Put fear aside and proceed.
Obstacles are there to strengthen you.
Remember:
The lie behind fear
is that you are alone and unprotected.
The truth is that I am with you always[6]
and I am your protection.[7]
I, the God who created the galaxies,[8]
am with you, guiding and protecting you.
Fear me only, so you can be free.

---

[1] Psalm 46:10a (ESV).
[2] Psalm 46:10a (ESV).
[3] Matthew 6:25-34; 1 Peter 5:7.
[4] Matthew 10:28-31.
[5] Psalm 138:8 (NLT).
[6] Matthew 28:20b.
[7] Psalm 18:2.
[8] Genesis 1:1; Isaiah 40:26; Psalm 33:6.

January 29

My treasure, my love:
I am not on the periphery of your life,
observing what is happening.
I am in the midst of you,[1]
intimately involved in every detail.
I am causing you to make choices
that lead you to fulfill your destiny.[2]
It's all good, my love.
You can relax about everything.
In fact, what would be best
would be for you to enjoy everything!
You might as well – I've got it all in hand.[3]
I'm planning every detail and executing every event.
Your job is to enjoy what's happening.
So let go of everything that is negative and be grateful.
Be grateful and rejoice,[4] my treasure.

---

[1] Zechariah 2:10; Zephaniah 3:17.
[2] Philippians 2:13.
[3] Psalm 138:8 (NLT); Colossians 1:16-17.
[4] Hebrews 12:28; 1 Thessalonians 5:17.

January 30

My child:

I love you.[1]

I "rejoice over you with singing."[2]

My desire for you

is that you experience fullness of joy

in my presence.[3]

I want you to have hilarious confidence in me

and my ability to be Lord.

I **am** Lord.[4]

Choose to believe this.

If you choose not to believe this,

it does not change the reality that I **am** Lord.

So why not believe it and be saved from worry?

The devastation of worry!

Choose to believe that I am Lord

and then let joy flow in and through you.[5]

Let "Jesus is Lord" be your motto, your theme, your salvation.

---

[1] 1 John 4:16.
[2] Zephaniah 3:17 (NIV).
[3] Psalm 16:11.
[4] Romans 14:11; Philippians 2:9-11.
[5] 1 Peter 1:8; Romans 15:13; Acts 16:34.

January 31

Dear friend:
You see enemies everywhere.
You see danger everywhere.
I see situations I am using
to test you and refine you and prune you.[1]
Persons through whom adversity comes are not your enemies.
Neither they, nor the situations they create,
are a danger to you or to be feared.
They simply are instruments in my hands
to purify and transform you.
I am painstakingly transforming you to be just like me.[2]
Have you not said you want to think like me:
to have my mind, to speak like me, to act like me?
Well, I am answering that prayer.
This situation you are in –
I was tempted in exactly the same way when I lived on earth.[3]
When you are on earth, earthly realities loom large
and heavenly realities seem faint and distant and elusive.
This is a distortion.
Earthly realities, at best, are a dim reflection of the eternal. What
happens on earth is inconsequential
except for the way in which God's glory is revealed through it.
I am revealing my glory through you in this situation.
Not once have you desired to retaliate.
You have continued to be respectful and considerate.
You have turned your cheek.
My treasure, my lovely: the heavenly hosts see this
and marvel at the power of my Spirit within you.[4]
So do not lose heart. And do not fear.
This trial will end.

---

[1] Psalm 66:10; Isaiah 48:10; 1 Peter 1:6-7.
[2] Romans 8:29; 2 Corinthians 3:17-18.
[3] Hebrews 4:15.
[4] Ephesians 3:20.

February

February 1

"Be still, and know that I am God."[1]
My child, you are in the palm of my hand.[2]
Lift up your heart and rejoice because you live in my love.[3]
Think of it: you live in my love.
You live in my love!
What can possibly harm you?
There is nothing that can separate you from my love.[4]
So be calm and be happy
and "(be) still and know that I am God."[5]

---

[1] Psalm 46:10a (ESV).
[2] Isaiah 49:2; Isaiah 51:16; Isaiah 62:3.
[3] 1 John 4:15-16.
[4] Romans 8:38-39.
[5] Psalm 46:10a (ESV).

February 2

My treasure:
Every day I wait for you to enter the quiet place
and spend some time paying attention to me.[1]
I **always** am waiting for this –
just like the father in the story of the prodigal son.[2]
I am waiting and longing to embrace you
in the intimacy of that hour.

---

[1] Mark 1:35.
[2] Luke 15:11-31.

February 3

My treasure, my love:
Let me show you
what is in my heart.
Let me show you
how I long for my people to be set free.[1]
The cares of this world
are choking the life out of my people.[2]
How hard it is
to seek first the Kingdom of God
in the midst of wealth![3]
Nevertheless, my love is stronger.[4]
I am calling my people out of this culture
of avarice and greed and lust.
I am calling and purifying a people
who will have a peculiar disinterest
in the accumulation of wealth
and a singular interest and delight
in building my Kingdom.[5]

---

[1] Isaiah 48:17-18; Deuteronomy 5:29 (NLT).
[2] Mark 4:19.
[3] Luke 18:24-25.
[4] 1 Corinthians 13:8.
[5] Matthew 6:33.

February 4

My treasure, my lovely one—
Be happy today.[1]
You can afford to be happy.
Why?
Because **I** am your God.
Think of it!!
The God who created the heavens and the earth is your God![2]
There is nothing on earth that you should fear.
There is nothing in heaven that you should fear.
Your lot is simply to enjoy each day
and all the blessings I continually provide.[3]

---

[1] Philippians 4:4; 1 Thessalonians 5:16.
[2] Genesis 1:1; Colossians 1:16.
[3] 1 Timothy 6:17.

February 5

My treasure:
Do not let your heart be troubled.[1]
I am your Shepherd[2] and I am guiding you.[3]
Your life is one ongoing transition
that ends with transition from life on earth to life in heaven.
So the challenge
is to learn to thrive
in the midst of transition and change.
You may feel ungrounded,
and you **are** ungrounded in earthly realities.
However, you are solidly grounded in me.[4]
Yes, you are solidly grounded in me!
Meditate on that fact
and you will find it easier to navigate all the changes.
Do not doubt that I am at work in you,
causing you to will and do my purpose.[5]
So relax and enjoy the ride.
I'm in charge and I know what I'm doing.
In the end, you will see it and be amazed.

---

[1] John 14:27.
[2] Psalm 23; John 10:11,14.
[3] Isaiah 58:11; John 16:13; Psalm 32:8 (NLT).
[4] Ephesians 3:16-19.
[5] Philippians 2:13.

February 6

My treasure:

Smile.

Smile expectantly because you are pregnant.

Yes!

You are pregnant with the plans I have for you.[1]

They are gestating within you.

I am forming them deep within you.[2]

Relax and smile expectantly

because they have been conceived

and they will come to full term

and be delivered.

When a woman is pregnant,

the best she can do is to look after herself

to support her gestation.

The same applies here.

Nurture your relationship with me and wait.

Wait patiently.

Wait expectantly.

Wait joyfully.

I am God.

---

[1] Jeremiah 29:11; Psalm 138:8 (NLT); Philippians 1:6; Ephesians 2:10.
[2] Philippians 2:13.

February 7

My child:
Look to me and live.
I take your face in my hands and cover it with kisses.
You are so precious to me![1]
Now then, about your concern for others:
Changing people's hearts is my department, my forte.[2]
I do it by revealing truth to them.[3]
Sometimes they receive it; sometimes they don't.
I respect their right to choose to walk away from the truth.
Search for the truth that will set people free,[4]
speak that truth in love,
and leave the results with me.

---

[1] Isaiah 43:4; Zephaniah 3:17.
[2] Psalm 51:10; Ezekiel 36:26; 2 Corinthians 5:17.
[3] John 16:13.
[4] John 8:32.

February 8

My dear child:
Throw away any notion of condemnation from me.
I do not condemn.
I did not send my Son to condemn the world
but to save it through love.[1]
Trust me.
Trust my love.[2]
Learn to be sensitive to my Spirit
who provides little "checks" in your spirit
when you are beginning to resist my love.[3]
Enjoy this day, my love.
Trust me work out all the details for you.[4]
Rest in my love, my darling.
Be nurtured and healed in my warm embrace.

[1] John 3:17.
[2] Psalm 52:8; 1 John 4:16.
[3] Romans 8:9; Ephesians 5:17-18.
[4] Psalm 138:8 (NLT).

February 9

My treasure:

"The earth is the LORD's and the fullness thereof..."[1]
That means that all things are mine.
All things were created by me and for me.[2]
So do not fear anything that has been created.
I can use all things, and do so as I see fit.[3]
Do not fear.[4]
Fear is one of the tactics of the deceiver.
Live by faith:

- Faith in my sovereignty,
- Faith in my love,
- Faith in my Word,
- Faith in my justice,
- Faith in my guidance,
- Faith in my provision,
- Faith in my character,
- Faith in my salvation...

That pesky fly, Satan, has been tormenting you with fear for many years. But now you are onto this. Stand strong in my life within you, and resist this oppression[5] with the fly swatter I have given you – my Word![6]

---

[1] Psalm 24:1a (ESV).
[2] Genesis 1:1; Colossians 1:16.
[3] Romans 8:28.
[4] Isaiah 41:10; Isaiah 43:1; Psalm 27:1.
[5] James 4:7.
[6] As exemplified by Jesus in Luke 4:1-13.

February 10

My precious, darling child:
I love you.[1]
I love you more than you ever can know.
With great care I created you.[2]
I love everything about you.[3]
I'm delighted with so much about you,
I hardly know where to begin affirming you![4]
My darling child, Draw close to me[5] and be nurtured.
My treasure:
Keep your life simple.
Do the things you are inspired to do
and forget about the rest.[6]
Let me do all your worrying
because I'm the one who can do something
about the things that trouble you.[7]
I love you, my treasure, I love you.
Be comforted, my love.[8]
I am your mother; I am your father.[9]
You came from me and you will return to me.[10]
I am your life, your source, your hope, and your joy.[11]
Rejoice and be exceedingly glad
because I am your God and I am your all.

---

[1] Ephesians 1:4-5; 1 John 4:9-10.
[2] Psalm 139:13-16; Isaiah 44:24.
[3] Genesis 1:31.
[4] Psalm 149:4; Zephaniah 3:17 (NLT).
[5] James 4:8a.
[6] Philippians 2:13.
[7] Psalm 55:22; 1 Peter 5:7.
[8] 2 Corinthians 1:3-4.
[9] John 1:12-13; Isaiah 49:15; 2 Corinthians 6:18.
[10] John 13:3.
[11] Job 33:4; Psalm 16:2; Psalm 62:5; Psalm 43:4.

February 11

My treasure, my dearest:
I am your shield.[1]
I am your glory.[2]
I am the lifter of your head.[3]
I am your life and your all.[4]
So relax and enjoy this communion.
Know that I am pleased to be your life and your all.

---

[1] Psalm 3:3.
[2] Psalm 3:3.
[3] Psalm 3:3.
[4] Job 33:4; Galatians 2:20, Colossians 3:4.

February 12

My treasure, my love:
Let my joy be in you today.[1]
Choose to make a way for that joy.[2]
Breathe deeply.
Smile.
Imagine this joy bubbling up and overflowing
out of the expansiveness in your heart
where you and I live in complete oneness.
Yes, my love, complete oneness.
Jesus in you, I in Jesus, the three of us –
and four, together with the Holy Spirit –
in complete oneness.[3]
In this oneness
there is only love, and joy, and peace, and power.
Let this oneness pervade your being,
and let it flow out to the world.
In the ritual of communion, you celebrate this oneness.
My treasure, meditate on our oneness
and let your being flow out of that life.

---

[1] Isaiah 29:19 (NLT).
[2] John 15:9-17.
[3] John 17:20-23.

February 13

My treasure:

I am looking at you and smiling, my child, because today, when I went for chemotherapy, you sat with me and held my hand.[1]

I know that you wanted to take your friend by the hand, to say "Be healed!" and to see me heal her. But you did exactly what I wanted you to do today.

And did you notice how I arranged it so you showed up at exactly the right time? You are a yielded vessel in my hands.[2]

I am looking at you and smiling![3]

---

[1] Matthew 25:40.
[2] Ephesians 2:10.
[3] Psalm 67:1.

February 14

My treasure, my love:

"Do not let your heart be troubled..."[1]

I am God. I am **your** God.[2]

Your sins are nailed to the cross of Christ and you stand before me, holy and blameless, without a single fault.[3]

I have cancelled the record that contained the charges against you. I took it and destroyed it by nailing it to the cross of Christ.[4]

In this way, I disarmed the evil rulers and authorities; I shamed them publicly by my victory over them on the cross of Christ.[5]

So do not let anyone condemn you.

You have overcome the accuser by the blood of the Lamb.[6]

Your sins – past, and present and future – and all charges made against you – past, present and future – all are nailed to the cross.

So, you do not need to be perfect. You can make mistakes. You will sin sometimes. Don't worry about this because I have taken care of this for you in advance.

So you really can relax.

When accusations come, remind yourself that all charges laid against you have been cancelled by the cross of Christ. That enemy has been disarmed, rendered impotent, and publicly shamed by the cross of Christ.

When accusations come, let them slide by you and end up on the cross.

And be thankful for what Jesus did for you on that cross.

---

[1] John 14:1a (New American Standard Bible – NASB).
[2] Joel 2:27.
[3] Colossians 1:21-22 (NLT); Ephesians 1:4-5.
[4] Colossians 2:13-14.
[5] Colossians 2:15.
[6] Revelation 12:11.

February 15

My treasure:
I speak to you from that cornerstone place,
that bedrock of your existence deep within your spirit.[1]
I have set up my throne there –
Yes, the throne with "the glow of an emerald
(encircling it) like a rainbow."[2]
Yes, the throne with the flashes of lightening
and the rumble of thunder.[3]
And yes, the throne with the power to heal,
the power to serve,
and the power to love extravagantly.[4]
Your focus, my love,
is to stay close to me for your life, at its best,
flows out of our intimacy within that throne room.
Right now you are feeling fear.
That fear does not come from me.
I give you "…a spirit…of power, and of love,
and of wise discretion"[5] –
not fear!
Resist fear with love – [6]
Be filled with my love and extend that love to all.[7]

---

[1] Matthew 7:24-27.
[2] Revelation 4:3b (NIV).
[3] Revelation 4:5.
[4] Demonstrated in the life of Christ who came from the throne of God, e.g.,
Luke 5:17, John 13:1-17, Romans 5:7-8.
[5] 2 Timothy 1:7 (Darby Bible Translation – DBT).
[6] Ephesians 3:19.
[7] Ephesians 5:2.

February 16

My treasure, my love:

Do not be troubled.[1]

Trust in my love and my goodness and my delight in you.

I have begun a good work in you

and I have every intention of completing it.[2]

My treasure: rest in me.

Rest in me, my love.

Lean on me.

Let me give you rest.[3]

I am getting off my throne,

coming to meet you,

and wrapping my strong arms around you.

I am bending over,

kissing the top of your head,

and reassuring you that all is well.

All is well, my precious one.

There is no condemnation, no recrimination, no shame –

only love and acceptance and joy.[4]

Now go.

Enjoy your day.

Why be downcast?

I am your God, your hope, your everything![5]

So rejoice.

Be glad.

Don't waste this day wallowing in sorrow!

---

[1] John 14:1.
[2] Philippians 1:6.
[3] Matthew 11:28-30.
[4] Romans 8.
[5] Psalm 42:11.

You are forgiven and made righteous:
holy, pure, blameless, faultless.
Give me all your concerns, let them all go, and just be happy.
That is my will for you today:
Be happy![1]
Be happy, my treasure.
Celebrate my joy within you.[2]
Laugh today.
Be done with seriousness.
The battle is mine, not yours, and I have won it![3]

---

[1] Ecclesiastes 3:12.
[2] Psalm 43:4-5.
[3] 1 Samuel 14:47.

February 17

My child, my delight:

You know, of course, that the best preparation for everything is to remain in the Vine.[1]

So let go of everything that is not righteousness, peace, and joy.[2]

Take it off – as grave clothes.[3]

If you have done that, and you continue to experience something other than righteousness, peace, and joy, consider whether you need to repent of sin, or whether you are being oppressed by the enemy.

My will is for you to experience my righteousness, peace, and joy at all times.

I am leading you, one step at a time, to a new place of fruitfulness. Enjoy the journey, my child, and laugh at any obstacles that appear.

Indeed, these obstacles are "apparent" obstacles – obstacles in appearance only, for I have allowed them as part of my plan.[4]

Now then, to get specific:

When something you were anticipating gets canceled, rejoice! I am behind this.

When someone you were counting on does not follow through, rejoice! I am using this.

When things break down, rejoice! I have a purpose in this.

When there's a seemingly negative message, rejoice! I am doing something.

---

[1] John 15:1-17.
[2] Romans 14:17.
[3] John 11:44.
[4] Psalm 138:8 (NLT); Romans 5:3-5; James 1:2-4; 1 Peter 4:12-13.

Just as Jesus knew that everything that happened in his life was in my hands, so you can know that everything that happens in your life is in my hands.

The life of Jesus within you, your life in the Spirit,[1] knows this and is perfectly relaxed about all that is happening and all that will happen.

Remain in the Vine.

---

[1] John 14:23; John 17:23; Romans 8:10; Galatians 2:20; Ephesians 3:16.

February 18

My love, my treasure:

Drink deeply of my love and enter into my rest.[1]

Remain in me[2] and I will guide you every step of the way.[3]

Here are the signs of remaining in me:

peace, joy, love, hope, patience, kindness, faithfulness, goodness, gentleness, and self-control.

In other words, all the fruit of the Spirit plus hope.[4]

If you are not experiencing these,

then you need to confess and repent of sin,[5]

or resist the devil,[6]

or bring something to me in prayer,[7]

or travail in intercession,[8]

or any combination of these.

And when you have done this,

then stand and wait for my deliverance.[9]

All is well, my love.

All is well.

---

[1] Matthew 11:28-30.

[2] John 15:4.

[3] Isaiah 58:11; Psalm 32:8 (NLT); Psalm 73:23-26; Proverbs 4:11-12; Proverbs 3:5-6.

[4] Galatians 5:22-23.

[5] Acts 3:19.

[6] James 4:7.

[7] Philippians 4:6.

[8] 1 Timothy 2:1.

[9] 2 Chronicles 20:17; 1 Corinthians 15:58.

February 19

Beautiful child:
I have received all your thoughts and prayers and questions.[1]
I am holding them close to my heart.
When the time is right,
I will send the answers.[2]
You have done your part,
as you responded to the nudging of my Spirit within you,[3]
and now you can rest,
knowing that I have these things in hand.[4]

---

[1] 2 Samuel 22:7.
[2] Psalm 120:1.
[3] Galatians 5:25.
[4] Philippians 4:6-7; Isaiah 26:3.

February 20

My treasure, my love:
You are not understanding our oneness:
Jesus in you and me in Jesus.[1]
In your life – body, soul and spirit – it is just as Jesus prayed.[2]
So have confidence
that any thoughts that bring life
are from me.
Have confidence that any thoughts
that are in sync with scripture are from me.
Dream, my child.
Dream big dreams!
Dream dreams that are totally impossible to accomplish
apart from the power of my Spirit.[3]
Dream dreams that bring life and hope and peace and justice
to this hurting world.
Dream, my love, because in your dreams I am telling you
what I am doing and the role I am asking you to fulfill.[4]
My treasure, I am laying in you a solid foundation
on which to build this dream.
So carry on!
Live each day to the max,
believing for the impossible,
hoping and trusting in me,
and just being happy.
I love you, my child.
I have carefully been shaping you for this time.
"Be still, and know that I am God."[5]
"Be still, and know that I am God."[6]

---

[1] 1 John 4:15; John 14:23; Revelation 3:20.
[2] John 17:20-23.
[3] Jeremiah 32:7; Luke 18:27; Matthew 19:26.
[4] Numbers 12:6; Acts 2:16-18.
[5] Psalm 46:10a (ESV).
[6] Psalm 46:10a (ESV).

February 21

My treasure, my love:
You have nothing to fear.
I am your Shepherd and I am looking after all your needs.[1]
Respond to everything with thanksgiving[2]
and worry about nothing.[3]
Laugh in the face of lack, my love.[4]
Literally laugh!
Lack is a great imposter and has no place in your life.

---

[1] Psalm 23; John 10:11; Philippians 4:19.
[2] Ephesians 5:20; 1 Thessalonians 5:18.
[3] Matthew 6:25-34; Philippians 4:4-7.
[4] Proverbs 31:25 (NLT).

February 22

My treasure, my love:
Lean on me.[1]
Lean on me and enter into my rest.[2]
Enter into my rest because I have won the victory.[3]
All that is left to do, my love,
is to pick up the spoils,
to ransack the enemy's stronghold,
and to celebrate the victory
won by Jesus' death and resurrection.[4]
The work of salvation is finished.
It is fully accomplished, my love.
There is nothing you can do to add to it.
All you can do is accept it as a free gift of grace.
No action on your part will add one iota to your salvation.
Yes, thanksgiving and obedience and worship
are appropriate responses,
but they do not add to your salvation.
They may help you realize your salvation,
but they will not add to it.
Jesus has done it all.
So find yourself in him and rest.
Enjoy the ride as my Spirit takes you where I will.[5]
Remember that you always are in Jesus' triumphal procession – no
matter what is happening.[6]
Lift up your head, my treasure,
and smile because you are in a victory march.

---

[1] Psalm 62:7; Isaiah 50:10; 2 Corinthians 1:9.
[2] Hebrews 4:1-11; Matthew 11:28-30.
[3] John 16:33.
[4] Mark 3:22-29; Colossians 2:13-15.
[5] Philippians 2:13.
[6] 2 Corinthians 2:14.

February 23

My love, my treasure:
Know that your heart and mine beat as one –
we are totally in sync, you and I.[1]
My desires are your desires; your desires are my desires.
I am making a way for you
and I will show you how to walk in it.[2]
My love, you have come to me again and again
with the request to live a life that imitates that of Jesus.
I have heard this and I have instigated it.[3]
My intention is to do it.
So continue to lift your face up to me.
Continue to receive my love.
Know that I am cradling your face in my hands,
I am smiling into your eyes,
and I am blowing you kisses all the time.
And when I'm not doing that,
I'm singing happy songs over you![4]
I delight in you,[5] my child!
Rest in my love
and wait to see my Spirit at work in and through you
to bless this hurting world.

---

[1] 1 John 4:15; John 17:20-23.
[2] Jeremiah 29:11; Psalm 32:8 (NLT); Psalm 73:23-26.
[3] Romans 8:26-27.
[4] Zephaniah 3:17 (NLT).
[5] Psalm 22:8.

February 24

My love, my treasure:
Be still in my presence[1] and let me speak to you.
I want to give you what you want.
Let this truth become real to you:
I want to give you what you want.
Is it not written, "Delight yourself in the Lord,
and He will give you the desires of your heart?"[2]
Well, that is my intention.
I am quite delighted to give you what you desire
because you have been delighting yourself in me.
Don't think I haven't noticed this!
I have seen this and I am so pleased to give you the Kingdom.[3]
My love, my treasure:
You need to be careful what you ask for
because I will give it to you![4]
Maybe not exactly how and when you are thinking,
but give it to you I will!
So be at peace.
Settle into what you want to do.
Pay attention to your desires.
Ask me for anything you wish.
And have a blast, loving and serving me!
I will give you anything you need to do whatever you want.
Just keep delighting yourself in me, and all will be well.
All **is** well.
You are deeply loved.
Stand tall in your place as my child – my treasured child.[5]
My treasured child.

---

[1] Psalm 37:7a; Psalm 62:5.
[2] Psalm 37:4 (ESV).
[3] Luke 12:32; Jeremiah 32:41a (NLT).
[4] John 16:23.
[5] 1 John 3:1; Romans 8:15-16; John 1:12.

February 25

My treasure, my love:
I am at work in you,
cleansing you from all unrighteousness[1]
and using you to build my Kingdom
even while I am doing this work of sanctification.
Everything that happens in your life serves my purposes.[2]
One of the areas of my cleansing work
concerns your tendency to resist what I provide.
This resistance causes grief for you.
Receive the grace to repent of this.

---

[1] Ephesians 5:25-27; 1 Corinthians 6:11; 2 Thessalonians 2:13.
[2] Romans 8:28; Ephesians 1:11; Psalm 37:23; Isaiah 46:10.

February 26

My treasure, my love:
You can trust me to motivate you to do my will.[1]
I motivate you to do all kinds of things –
like baking cookies, for example.
Yes, I motivate you to do even the mundane things in life.
Frankly, nothing is mundane to me.
Everything is precious.
I love everything about human existence.
I created it and every detail of it gives me great joy![2]

---

[1] Philippians 2:13.
[2] Genesis 1:31; Psalm 104:31.

February 27

My love, my treasure:
I see your low place.
I am with you in that low place.[1]
Be at peace there because I am with you.
This is a temporary place –
you will again have energy and enthusiasm.
In the meantime, rest in me.[2]
Do not resist this. Rest in me.

---

[1] Isaiah 41:10; Isaiah 43:2; Matthew 28:20b.
[2] Matthew 11:28-29.

February 28

My love, my treasure:
You can afford to be at rest
because I am looking after everything for you.[1]
You are wondering
how you are going to find out what I have planned.
Well, I have a multitude of ways of communicating this to you!
For example, I like to guide you through scripture.[2]
I like to put my desires for you in your heart
and then give you the desires of your heart.[3]
In addition, I lead through circumstances.
I also lead through the word of knowledge.[4]
Sometimes I have others speak my Word to you.[5]
Frankly, I can use anything
to communicate my plan and my will to you.
Do you remember the time I spoke to you through a movie?
And there are countless times
when I have guided you through something you have read.
So relax, my love.
I am making my way clear to you in a timely fashion.
As for this thing that is troubling you,
leave that in my hands.[6]
Just let it go.

---

[1] Matthew 6:25-34.
[2] Psalm 119:105.
[3] Psalm 37:4; Psalm 20:4.
[4] 1 Corinthians 12:8.
[5] Proverbs 17:22; Ecclesiastes 12:11.
[6] Psalm 55:22; 1 Peter 5:7.

February 29

My treasure, my love:
Put your hope in me and lean on me.[1]
Do not be discouraged or dismayed.
Put your hope in me.
Put your hope in me.
Put your hope in me and rest.[2]
You are acting as though I am not Lord of all.[3]
You are acting as though I am not good.[4]
You are acting
as though I have not heard your cries.[5]
You are acting
as though I do not know the desires of your heart.[6]
No, my love.
This is not the behavior of a child of Royalty.[7]
Put your crown back on and rest in who you are.
Rest in **whose** you are.
Rest and enjoy where you are now,
knowing that I am looking after your future.[8]
It is a future fit for the child of Royalty.
I have paid the price[9] for you to rest on my laurels.
So rest, my love.
Rest in me and enjoy each day as it comes from my hand.

---

[1] Psalm 42; Psalm 25:5 (NLT); 1 Timothy 6:17.
[2] Matthew 11:28-30.
[3] Romans 10:12; Acts 10:36.
[4] Psalm 100:5; Psalm 135:3; 1 Peter 2:2-3.
[5] Psalm 116:1; 1 John 5:14.
[6] Psalm 20:4; Psalm 37:4.
[7] 1 John 3:1-2; 2 Corinthians 6:18.
[8] Jeremiah 29:11
[9] 1 Corinthians 7:23.

March

March 1

My treasure, my love:
Let me speak to your worried heart.
Let me speak to your hurting heart.
I want you to know that what is happening in your life
is happening because I am answering your prayer
for intimacy with me.
All of these things are helping to remove barriers between us.
All of these circumstances also are increasing your faith –
increasing and purifying it.[1]
I am bringing you to the place
where you know that you know nothing.
When you are there –
at this place of being poor in spirit –
you will experience the fullness of my presence within you.[2]
Yes. And then you will experience
the power of my presence within you.
My treasure, my love:
I have inspired you to pray these prayers
and I surely am answering them.[3]
I am pleased to be answering them![4]
My love:
You are really going to enjoy these next years.
Yes, you **are** going to enjoy them.
I know you have a hard time comprehending this
because you have experienced life as being very difficult.
That's because you haven't learned how to rest.[5]
But I am teaching you that, too.
Yes, with me **all** things are possible—even that![6]

---

[1] Romans 5:3-5; James 1:2-4; 1 Peter 4:12-13.
[2] Isaiah 57:15; Matthew 5:3.
[3] 2 Corinthians 6:2; 1 John 5:14-15.
[4] Jeremiah 32:41a (NLT).
[5] Isaiah 30:15.
[6] Matthew 19:26; Luke 1:37; Genesis 18:14; Jeremiah 32:17.

March 2

My love, my treasure:
I am delighted to give you everything you need.[1]
Give yourself permission to imagine exactly what you need
and then ask.
Ask and believe you will receive.[2]
And remember – I already have given you all you need.
From my viewpoint,
you already have received everything you need.
This all is already written in my Book of Life[3] –
you just haven't experienced it yet!
When you think of the future,
think in terms of "What **has** God given me?"
rather than "What **will** God give me?"
My treasure, my love:
If only you could grasp how deeply I love you![4]
If only you could know
how extravagantly I have provided for you![5]
If only you could peek into the fabulous future
I have planned for you![6]
Then your worrying days would be over!
So take heart and plan.
Plan and ask.
Ask and believe.
Believe and receive.
Receive and rejoice.

---

[1] Psalm 23:1; 2 Corinthians 9:8; Matthew 6:33.
[2] Matthew 21:22; Mark 11:24; 1 John 5:15.
[3] Psalm 139:16; Philippians 4:3; Revelation 3:5; Revelation 20:12.
[4] Ephesians 3:16-19; Romans 5:7-8.
[5] 1 Corinthians 2:9; Psalm 31:19.
[6] Jeremiah 29:11; 2 Timothy 2:12; Romans 8:17; 1 Peter 5:4.

Yes, **rejoice**!
Rejoice **now** because I am your doting parent
and you are my cherished child!
I have given you my life and my love forever.
I love you, my child.
I love you deeply and extravagantly and passionately.
You are mine and I am yours.[1]
There is no need to be anxious about anything.[2]
Instead, be excited!
Be excited in anticipation
of how you will experience my provision.

---

[1] Song of Solomon 6:3.
[2] Matthew 6:25-34.

March 3

My love, my treasure:

You are the apple of my eye![1]

I really have enjoyed the last few hours

we have spent working together.[2]

My love, I urge you to practice patience.[3]

Moses knew his life purpose when he was forty,

but it took another forty years of wilderness living

before he was ready.

It took that long before the Israelites were ready.

Moses was eighty when he moved into his leadership role.[4]

So, relax and enjoy what I have given you to do now.

I know what is in your heart – have I not placed it there?[5]

It is like a seed that is germinating under the earth,

a child in gestation,

a butterfly in a cocoon.

I will not allow it to be revealed until it is ready.

I will not allow it to be manifest until the time is ready.

Invest the talent I have given you now and at just the right time, I

will give you more.[6]

Yes, my intention is to give you the desire of your heart.[7]

One day you will find yourself living that dream.

Furthermore, I am not upset about your age.

I am not impatient with your progress.

---

[1] Psalm 17:8; Proverbs 7:2; Deuteronomy 32:10; Zechariah 2:8.

[2] 1 Corinthians 3:9; 2 Corinthians 6:1.

[3] Colossians 1:11; Hebrews 6:12; 2 Peter 1:5-7 (NLT).

[4] The story of Moses is told in the book of Exodus. For a summary of the life of Moses, see Acts 7:20-44.

[5] Hebrews 13:20-21; Philippians 2:13

[6] Matthew 25:14-30.

[7] Psalm 37:4; Psalm 20:4.

I am not frustrated that you are not doing today
what I have planned for tomorrow.
The challenge, my love, is to live this day to the max,
to enjoy this day to the max,
to celebrate this day to the max.
Tomorrow is tomorrow – it can't be lived today.
The best way to prepare for tomorrow is to really live today.
So live this day, my love.
Live the life of my Son today.[1]
I love you, my treasure.
Live and be in my love for you.[2]

---

[1] Galatians 2:20.
[2] John 15:9-17.

March 4

My love, my treasured child:
You are wondering whether or not I have something
that I want to say to you today.
The truth is that I **always** have something to say to you![1]
I **always** am speaking to you!
I speak through my Word,
through circumstances, through other people –
I am able to speak through anything!
And I also speak through silence –
sometimes the strongest message I give is through silence.
So listen to the voice of my Spirit, my love.[2]
And celebrate my presence within you, my love.[3]
Bask in my love for you.[4]
Because you have my presence, you have all you need.
Because you have my presence, you lack nothing –
even when you are experiencing physical hunger,
even when you are experiencing inadequate funds,
even when you are experiencing confusion or uncertainty,
even when you are experiencing sorrow…
Celebrate my presence within you.
Celebrate my love within you.
Celebrate my joy within you.[5]
Celebrate my peace within you.[6]
And celebrate my power within you.[7]
Know that today I will enable you
to do everything I have planned for you.[8]

---

[1] Job 33:14.
[2] Isaiah 55:3
[3] John 14:23; Romans 8:11.
[4] Romans 5:5; Jude 1:21; 2 Thessalonians 3:5.
[5] John 15:11.
[6] John 14:27; John 16:33; Colossians 3:15.
[7] Ephesians 1:18-20
[8] Philippians 2:13; Hebrews 13:21.

March 5

My treasure, my love:
Let it all go – all these things you are puzzling over.[1]
Let it all go because I am looking after it all.[2]
You can laugh and relax.
Truly, you can.
I am going to cause everything to happen
in the perfect way
at the perfect time.
So just let it all go.
All you need to do is to expect me to be your detail person.
I have planned it all from beginning to end.
It is all written in my book.[3]
Rejoice and let go, my love.
Let go.

---

[1] Psalm 131.
[2] Hebrews 1:3a; Colossians 1:16-17.
[3] Psalm 139:16.

March 6

I say that it is time for you to stand tall.
I say that it is time for you to stand strong.[1]
I say that it is time for you
to take that territory back from the enemy.
No more being a puff cake!
You know your authority. Stand in that authority.[2]
You know who you are. Take my scepter and rule.[3]
Just as Moses picked up his rod
and struck the water to make a path[4]
and struck the rock[5] to make water,
so you are to pick up my scepter
and command things into being.
Now is the time, my love.
Now is the time.

---

[1] Ephesians 6:10-17.
[2] Luke 10:19.
[3] Luke 22:29-30; 2 Timothy 2:12.
[4] Exodus 13:17-14:31.
[5] Exodus 17:1-7.

March 7

My love, my treasure:
"Be still, and know that I am God."[1]
I am your source.[2]
Even when you are not thinking about me, I am within you —
a spring of life-giving water bubbling up and infusing you.[3]
Drink deeply of this water of life, my love.[4]
You are thinking of disappointments. Stop doing this.
It keeps you from enjoying the blessings of today.
In addition, my will for you is unfolding and will unfold,
even when you are not aware of it.
"Be still, and know that I am God" [5]
and I am causing your life to unfold as I have ordained.[6]

---

[1] Psalm 46:10a (ESV).
[2] Psalm 16:2.
[3] John 4:14; John 7:38.
[4] Revelation 7:16-17; Revelation 21:6; Revelation 22:1.
[5] Psalm 46:10a (ESV).
[6] Psalm 42:8; Psalm 32:8 (NLT); Philippians 2:13; Psalm 139:16.

March 8

My treasure, my love:
Thank you for once more turning your face towards mine.
You have been scrambling about
like a chicken with its head cut off!
It's been quite a frenzied dance we were having,
as I kept step with you!
I suggest the dance would be more elegant
if you were to let me lead.

You are wondering about taking a weeklong vacation
and have asked whether that is your idea or mine.
I like the idea.
It's a good idea.
It would please me for you to take a week off
because you would be demonstrating faith in doing so.
Faith!
That's what I'm looking for! That's what pleases me![1]

You have been troubled about the wellbeing of that one you love.
My love, my treasure: Leave that with me.
I am doing a work
that is requiring extensive firing in the kiln of adversity.[2]
Just like helping a butterfly leave a cocoon
thwarts its ability to fly,
in the same way,
lowering the heat or shortening the time in the kiln
would interfere with the process
of building strength and endurance.

---

[1] Hebrews 11:6.
[2] Romans 5:3-5; James 1:2-4.

So do not interfere with this process.
Respect it. Honor it. Support it.
You are concerned about where you will be next year.
I am going to make that clear to you in the fullness of time.[1]
In the meantime,
it would please me if you would trust me with this.[2]

Now then, I would like to talk to you about my love for you.
What can I say that will help you to know it, to rest in it?
I am demonstrating my love for you all the time.
Celebrate what I have done, my treasure,
and then you will be able to know and rest in my love.[3]

---

[1] Psalm 32:8 (NLT).
[2] Psalm 143:8.
[3] Psalm 40.

March 9

Dear friend:

Trust me.

Choose to trust me.

Choose to trust that I love you.

Choose to trust that my love is stronger than any fear.[1]

When fear engulfs you –

and engulf you it will –

remember that it cannot touch your spirit.

Your spirit has been reborn.[2]

"…(You) no longer live, but Christ lives in (you)."[3]

Go with your spirit; wean your soul.[4]

Wean your soul by making it submit to the Word of Christ.

You have not been given "a spirit of fear,

but of power, and love, and of a sound mind."[5]

My plan for you is not to allow you to experience disaster,

but to prosper you and to give you a hope and a future.[6]

---

[1] Isaiah 12:2.
[2] 1 Peter 1:23.
[3] Galatians 2:20a (NIV).
[4] Psalm 131:2.
[5] 2 Timothy 1:7 (New Heart English Bible – NHEB).
[6] Jeremiah 29:11.

March 10

My treasure, my love:
Lift up your heart and be glad![1]
Choose to be glad, my love.[2]
Live in that place of joy
that comes from expressing gratitude.[3]
Gratitude is a door to joy.
I will say it again:
Gratitude is a door to joy.

---

[1] Lamentations 3:41.
[2] Philippians 4:4; Psalm 68:3.
[3] Psalm 100.

March 11

My treasure, my love:
When you are going through a hard time,
it is difficult to see my hand at work.
The fact is, however, that I **am** at work.
I am guiding every detail of your life
and the lives of your loved ones.[1]
I am fulfilling my promise
to cause you to will and to do my pleasure.[2]
I am redeeming this situation.
I am bringing good out of it for you
because you love me
and because I love you.[3]
Lift up your head and be glad.
Yes, be **very** glad because I am God
and I am **your** God.
Put your hope in me
and you will not be disappointed
or put to shame.[4]

---

[1] Psalm 32:8 (NLT); Isaiah 48:17.
[2] Philippians 2:13.
[3] Romans 8:28.
[4] Romans 10:11; Isaiah 49:23.

March 12

My love:
Pay no attention to what others think of you.[1]
Their thoughts are a reflection of them
and not an accurate reflection of you.
They are not in a position to judge you
because they know so very little about your experience.
Take no thought about what others may be thinking.
When it comes right down to it, you belong to me.[2]
I am your creator,[3] sustainer,[4] Lord,[5] and judge.[6]
You are mine.
"Be still, (my love,) and know that I am God."[7]
Be still and know that I am looking after everything for you.
It is a waste of time for you to be concerned about anything—
including what others might be thinking.
Believe in me.[8]
Believe in my tender, loving care.
Believe in my sovereignty.
Believe that I am working in and through all things
to build my Kingdom.
Believe that I am causing you to will and to do my purpose.[9]

---

[1] Proverbs 29:25; Psalm 56:4; Psalm 118:6; Romans 8:31.
[2] 1 John 4:4; 1 Corinthians 3:23; 1 Peter 2:9.
[3] Isaiah 44:24; Psalm 139:13.
[4] Psalm 54:4; Psalm 145:14; Romans 8:28-31.
[5] Colossians 2:6.
[6] Ecclesiastes 12:13-14; Romans 2:16; 2 Corinthians 5:10; 1 Corinthians 4:5.
[7] Psalm 46:10a (ESV).
[8] John 14:1
[9] Philippians 2:13.

March 13

My love, my treasure:

I want you to know that I am with you on this journey.[1]

You may feel like these waters are sweeping you under.[2]

You may be experiencing this

as being choked by the cords of death.[3]

That's not how I see it.

I see it as a tactic of the enemy to destroy you.[4]

I, however, am ministering to you the truth

that will set you free.[5]

This will not destroy you.

Instead, I am using it to cleanse you

and purify you

and prepare you.[6]

"Be still, and know that **I am God!**"[7]

Let go of false pride and boast in me.[8]

I will see you through.

I will see your family through.

I will set your feet on a rock

and you will stand tall and strong.[9]

Wait.

Wait patiently.

Wait with hope in your heart.[1]

---

[1] Isaiah 41:10; Matthew 28:20b.

[2] Isaiah 43:2.

[3] Psalm 18:3-6; Psalm 116:1-6.

[4] Ephesians 6:10-12; 1 Peter 5:8-9.

[5] John 8:32.

[6] Psalm 66:10; 1 Peter 1:6-7.

[7] Psalm 46:10a (ESV, emphasis added).

[8] 1 Corinthians 1:31; Jeremiah 9:23-24; 2 Corinthians 10:17.

[9] Psalm 40:2.

March 14

My love, my treasure:
I am bringing you out of a long dark valley.[2]
Do not try to understand everything about this valley –
Just know that I have been transforming you.[3]
If it feels like what has been happening is confusing and unclear,
that would make sense
because the process has been a metamorphosis.
What happens inside a cocoon is mysterious and marvelous.
Trust this process that I have initiated and I am orchestrating.[4]

---

[1] Romans 8:25; Lamentations 3:25-26.
[2] Psalm 23:4.
[3] Romans 12:2.
[4] Psalm 62:8; Psalm 37:5; Psalm 47:7.

March 15

My love, my treasure:
Your life is the life of Christ.[1]
This means that you are fully surrendered to me.[2]
Put yourself in agreement with that fact.
Think about the fruit of being fully surrendered:
There is no fear, only hope.
There is no worry, only faith.
There is no resisting, only rejoicing.
My love, my treasure,
Enter into my rest.[3]
Let my Spirit carry you home.[4]

---

[1] Galatians 2:20; Ephesians 3:16-17.
[2] John 5:19; John 5:30; John 6:38.
[3] Hebrews 4:1-11; Matthew 11:28-30.
[4] 1 Peter 3:18.

March 16

My treasure, my love:
If you could apprehend
the magnitude of my love for you,
you would rest in me.[1]
Let me help you see it.
It is like the universe –
my love for you extends endlessly.
It is like the air in the atmosphere –
my love for you has no beginning and no end.
It is like the sun –
my love for you has the power to warm the coldest day
and to dispel the blackest darkness.
My love will carry you through this difficult place.
Look for the evidence of my love being demonstrated
in and through your life every day.

---

[1] Psalm 36:5; Psalm 103:11 (NLT); Ephesians 3:17-19; 2 Thessalonians 3:5.

March 17

My treasure, my love:
You are exactly where I want you to be.
I continuously am causing you to will and to do my purpose.[1]
So just relax and enjoy what I provide for you each day.
If you follow your desires,
you will find that I have placed them there.[2]
You also will find
that I have provided the means to fulfil those desires.[3]
So do not be afraid.
Live your life with gusto, enjoying all the details.
Let fear be a thing of the past, relegated to antiquity.[4]
See it encrusted in stone,
fossilised,
and rendered immobile and harmless.

---

[1] Philippians 2:13; 1 Corinthians 12:6; Psalm 32:8 (NLT).
[2] Psalm 37:4; Psalm 20:4.
[3] Hebrews 13:20-21.
[4] Isaiah 41:10; Romans 8:31; Psalm 27:1.

March 18

My love, my treasure:
Lift up your heart and be glad.
I have created you,[1]
chosen you,[2]
redeemed you,[3]
and equipped you.[4]
You are mine[5] and I am yours.[6]
Do you know this?
Do you really know that I am yours?
Yes, and I want it that way!
I want to be yours!
I want you to know that I am yours.
You can walk into this day (and any day)
knowing that I am yours.
This means that you and I can do anything.
We can set our hand to any task and accomplish it.
Put your hope in me and be glad.[7]

---

[1] Psalm 100:3; Ephesians 2:10.
[2] 1 Peter 2:9.
[3] Galatians 3:13; Romans 3:23-24.
[4] 2 Timothy 3:16-17; Hebrews 13:21.
[5] 1 Corinthians 3:23.
[6] Ezekiel 34:31; Isaiah 43:3; 2 Corinthians 6:18.
[7] Psalm 42; 1 Timothy 6:17.

March 19

My love, my treasure:
Everything you have done that was done in love[1]
was done to me and for me.[2]
Everything you have done that was done in love
was done to me and for me.
And I will say it a third time:
Everything you have done that was done in love
was done to me and for me.
I have given you all the people in your life
and you have been faithful to love and serve them.
In loving them, you are loving me.
I receive everything you have done as a gift of love for me.
You look at what you have done for others
and judge your effort to be inadequate.[3]
You look at the fruit of your labour
and wonder if your effort was wasted.
I want to assure you that none of your effort was wasted and your
reward lies with me.[4]
I also want to assure you that I am not troubled
by the inadequacy of your efforts.
I, not you, am their Provider.
It never was my intention
that you perfectly meet all of their needs for all time!
I gather together all of your acts of love and service
and hold them close,
cherishing them as gifts of love
from your heart to mine.
Thank you, my love, thank you!

---

[1] 1 Corinthians 16:14; Ephesians 5:2.
[2] 1 Corinthians 16:14; Matthew 25:31-40.
[3] Isaiah 49:4a.
[4] Isaiah 49:4b.

March 20

My love, my treasure:
The sky is the limit.
In other words,
you are limited only by what you can imagine.
And in fact, you are not even limited by that
because in me there are **no** limitations![1]
I am the God for whom **nothing** is impossible.[2]

---

[1] Ephesians 3:20.
[2] Mark 10:27; Jeremiah 32:17.

March 21

My treasure, my love:
I see how difficult it is for you to still and quiet your soul[1]
so you can be in my presence.
I'll remind you of the Zig Ziglar quote you like to share
with people you are encouraging:
"Anything worth doing is worth doing poorly—
until you can learn to do it well!"[2]
There are no shortcuts to intimacy with me.
It takes time and effort.
Out of this intimacy will come healing.
Out of this intimacy will come guidance and direction.
Out of this intimacy will come peace and joy.
Out of this intimacy will come meaning and purpose.
So come. Sit at my feet every day.
Let's share our hearts with each other.
As you do this, you will be preparing for the time
when you come to be with me.
These times of sharing will make effortless
the transition from this life to the next.

---

[1] Psalm 131:2; Psalm 62:1.
[2] Zig Ziglar (1926-2012) was an American salesman, author, motivational
speaker, and personal development coach. Retrieved from
https://www.goodreads.com/quotes/260715-anything-worth-doing-is-worth-
doing-poorly--until-you-can-learn.

March 22

My love, my delight:
In the springtime, everything is new.
It's a new beginning.
In my Spirit, it's always springtime.
I always am doing a new thing.[1]
I am doing a new thing in you.
I am doing a new thing through you.
So be glad.
You love spring!
It's springtime!

---

[1] Isaiah 43:19; Isaiah 42:9; 2 Corinthians 5:17.

March 23

My love, my treasure:
Notice my presence within you.[1]
Just be still and notice.[2]
Notice the peace I bring.
Notice the stillness.
Notice the hope I bring.
Notice the courage.
Notice the joy and the enthusiasm.
My love, my treasure, in me you have everything you need.[3]
This challenging place you are in will not last forever.
I am using it to shape your character and to grow your faith.[4]
I am using it to enhance our relationship.
It's true: There is a place of quiet rest near to my heart.[5]
That place of quiet rest, my love, is within you.
That's where my heart is.
You need look no farther than in your heart.
I have come to dwell in your heart.[6]
That is where I am and that is exactly where I want to be!
Rivers of living water flow from my heart within your heart:[7]
Rivers of peace,
Rivers of joy,
Rivers of courage,
Rivers of hope,
And rivers of enthusiasm.
Well, and rivers of healing!
So celebrate my life within you and live.
Live life to the fullest from this moment on.

---

[1] John 17:20-23; Revelation 3:20.
[2] Psalm 131:2; Psalm 62:1.
[3] Matthew 6:33; 1 John 2:27; 2 Corinthians 9:8; Hebrews 13:21.
[4] Romans 5:3-5; James 1:2-4; 1 Peter 4:12-13.
[5] Matthew 11:28-30; John 1:18 (NLT).
[6] John 17:20-23; 1 John 4:15; Revelation 3:20.
[7] John 7:38.

March 24

My love, my treasure:
You are the apple of my eye![1]
I treasure you and protect you and nurture you and heal you.[2]
An appropriate image of your life right now
is that of a kayak going through white water.
No need to worry –
it'll be a hair-raising ride,
but I've got things under control!
There's no time for complacency or the same old same old.
This is all about growth and change.
Hang on and enjoy the ride!

---

[1] Psalm 17:8; Proverbs 7:2; Zechariah 2:8.
[2] Zephaniah 3:17; Psalm 91; John 17:15; Hebrews 12:5-7; Isaiah 53:5; Romans 8:11.

March 25

My treasure, my love:

I am here with you.[1]

I have been with you through this entire experience.

I have been sustaining you.

Have no regrets.

If that knot in your side could speak, it would say, "Let it go."

Your job is to do your best and leave the results to me.[2]

You need to learn to let go of the results.

You need to learn that there will be times

when you perform perfectly

and things will appear to go wrong.

You need to learn that there will be times

when you do not perform perfectly

and things will appear to turn out right.

The wise choice is to leave the results to me.

So leave this thing with me.

You have no way of assessing what really happened there.

Trust that I am at work in this situation, bringing good out of it.[3]

Trust in my future grace.[4]

---

[1] Matthew 28:20b; Isaiah 43:2; 2 Timothy 4:17.
[2] Isaiah 49:4.
[3] Romans 8:28.
[4] John 1:16.

March 26

My treasure, my love:
I am with you in all your deliberations.[1]
We are deliberating together, my love.
We are asking the questions together.
I'm with you in this!
Asking the questions leads you to the answers.
Asking the questions makes a way
for you to live into the answers.
And live into the answers you will!
In the meantime,
enjoy to the max what I have given you today.
You are exactly where I want you to be,
doing what I have given you to do.[2]
All that remains
is for you to learn to be content
and to enjoy each day.[3]

---

[1] 1 John 2:27; John 16:13.
[2] Philippians 2:13.
[3] 1 Timothy 6:6.

March 27

My treasure, my love:
I am holding you in the palm of my hand.[1]
I am tenderly shaping you into a beautiful vessel for the future.[2]
In the meantime,
I am pleased to dwell in the beautiful vessel you are now.[3]
It's about being ever transformed
from one beautiful vessel into another!
Please recognize that right now
you are perfectly formed for my purposes.
Ten years ago you were perfectly formed for my purposes then –
and so on.
Does this mean you never make mistakes?
Not at all!
You have made many mistakes
and you will continue to err.
This does not trouble me in the least.
Neither does it thwart my purposes.
My plan and my purposes
are greater than your errors of omission or commission.[4]
So lift up your head, put your hand in mine, and boldly live![5]
All is well, my love.

---

[1] Isaiah 49:2; Isaiah 51:16; Isaiah 62:3.
[2] Jeremiah 18:1-6.
[3] 2 Corinthians 4:6-7.
[4] Psalm 138:8 (NLT).
[5] 2 Corinthians 3:12.

March 28

My treasure, my love:
"In my Father's house are many dwelling places…
I (am going) to prepare a place for you."[1]
In the meantime, enjoy every moment where you are.
I see your struggle.
Do not resist it.
It is in the struggle to get out of the cocoon
that the butterfly builds its strength.
This is a noble struggle. Embrace it.
I have placed in your heart my purpose for your life.[2]
Do not be afraid to search for it and find it.
You will find it where love compels you to go.[3]
Yes! You will find it where love compels you to go.

---

[1] John 14:2 (NASB).
[2] Ezekiel 36:26-27.
[3] John 13:34; 1 Corinthians 14:1; 1 Corinthians 16:14; Galatians 5:14; Ephesians 5:1-2.

March 29

My treasure, my love:
When you still and quiet your soul,[1]
you always will become aware of my presence.
That's because I'm always with you![2]
Today I want to assure you that I **will** do whatever you believe.[3]
Just as Jesus told the woman
who touched the hem of his garment
that her faith had healed her,[4]
so your faith will accomplish whatever you truly believe.
This is not because you are special – although you are!
Rather, it's because that's how I have designed things to be.
You are created in my image.[5]
When we speak, we create what we believe.[6]

---

[1] Psalm 131:2; Psalm 62:1.
[2] Matthew 28:20b.
[3] Mark 11:23; Matthew 21:22.
[4] Matthew 9:20-22.
[5] Genesis 1:27; Ephesians 4:24.
[6] Psalm 33:6; Hebrews 11:3.

March 30

My treasure, my love:
You are the apple of my eye![1]
I wish you could know how deeply I love you,[2]
but that's just impossible.
Why?
Because my love for you is too great for you to understand!
My love for you is so intense, so deep, so all-consuming
that no human being could understand it.
My love for you is so pure, so entirely unconditional
that no human being could comprehend it.
My love for you is so full of joy and delight
that it defies description.
Let my love wash away your tears.
Let my love wash away your fears.
Let my love wash away
all the negative programming
that you have received.
Let my love give you a new beginning, a fresh start.
Know that you are deeply, deeply loved.
Know that you are treasured.
Know that you are considered to be very precious.
Know that I long to bless you with every good thing.[3]
You are my dearly loved child.[4]

---

[1] Psalm 17:8; Proverbs 7:2; Zechariah 2:8; Deuteronomy 32:10.
[2] Psalm 36:5,7; Psalm 103:11; 2 Thessalonians 3:5; Ephesians 3:17-19.
[3] Psalm 23:1; James 1:17; Matthew 7:11; Romans 8:32.
[4] Ephesians 5:1; 1 John 3:1-2.

March 31

My treasure, my love:
Be set free
from all the limitations of your misbeliefs.[1]
Be healed.
Be set free
from all the inappropriate limitations and expectations
that others have placed on you.
Be healed.
Be set free to live the life I have planned for you
from before the foundations of the earth.[2]
Be set free to soar.
You are perfectly shaped
for that certain work I have prepared for you.[3]
I continuously am setting things up for each day's experience.[4]
Face each day with excitement and joy.[5]
Proceed through each day with excitement and joy.
I have gone ahead of you to prepare the way,
and I am with you throughout each day.[6]

---

[1] Romans 12:2; Ephesians 4:23; Colossians 3:10.
[2] Psalm 37:23; Psalm 138:8 (NLT); Ephesians 1:4.
[3] Ephesians 2:10.
[4] Deuteronomy 31:8.
[5] Philippians 4:4; 1 Thessalonians 5:16.
[6] Deuteronomy 31:8; Isaiah 41:10; Isaiah 43:2; Matthew 28:20b.

April

April 1

My treasure, my love:
Sometimes you need to look at a problem
from the corner of your eye rather than full on.
Sometimes peripheral vision reveals a clarity
that cannot be discerned in a direct gaze.
What do you see out of the corner of your eye?
What is there that has been dancing around the edges?
Those little blips on the horizon?
When the time is right,
I will show you the way[1]
and cause you to walk in it.[2]

---

[1] Psalm 32:8 (NLT); Isaiah 48:17.
[2] Philippians 2:13.

April 2

My treasure, my love:
Come sit up here with me.
Let's look down on your life
from this place in the heavenlies.[1]
What do you see?
I see my glory filling the universe.[2]
I see you perfectly positioned in the midst of my glory.
I am excited to see what is unfolding.
And it is unfolding just as I have ordained![3]
Let's just look at this, you and I.
From this perspective we can see all of eternity.
We can see how it all came from me
and how it all returns to me.
Remain in my love,[4] child of mine![5]
Remain immersed in my love.
Be motivated by my love[6]
and you will find your way.

---

[1] Ephesians 2:6.
[2] Isaiah 6:3.
[3] 2 Kings 19:25; Psalm 139:16.
[4] John 15:9.
[5] 1 John 5:1.
[6] 1 Corinthians 13.

April 3

My treasure, my love:
You really don't need to worry
about what you are doing with your life.
I've got that all in hand.[1]
First of all, where you are right now is perfect.
Just enjoy it.
In due time you will live into the other things
I have planned for you.[2]
Relax and let this unfold.
Relax and enjoy your place of joy, gratitude and love.
Just enjoy it, my love!

[1] Hebrews 1:3; Colossians 1:16-17.
[2] Psalm 32:8 (NLT); Ephesians 2:10.

April 4

My treasure, my love:
What joy I have in my heart when I commune with you![1]
What joy when I celebrate our oneness![2]
Today is the first day of the rest of your life –
a life that is characterized by contentment and joy
in knowing that we are enough.
You and I are enough.
We are more than enough!
Together we can do anything![3]
I am the resurrection, the way, the life, and the truth.[4]
"…I am the light of the world."[5]
And I choose to live in you![6]
I choose to live in you with all that I am![7]
My treasure, my love,
This is as I designed it.
I challenge you to believe it and to live it!

---

[1] Zephaniah 3:17; John 15:11.
[2] John 14:23; John 17:20-23; 1 John 4:15; Revelation 3:20.
[3] John 15:7,16; Philippians 4:13.
[4] John 11:25; John 14:6.
[5] John 9:5 (NLT).
[6] 1 Corinthians 3:16; 1 Corinthians 6:19; John 14:23.
[7] Colossians 1:19.

April 5

My treasure, my love:
Yes, yes, yes! Make joy your focus![1]
And why not?
This is exactly what the suffering of my Son
purchased on your behalf.[2]
It's there for you to receive.
It's there for you to enjoy.
Make joy your ordinary way of being.
And when you experience adversity,
make joy your weapon, your antidote, your default mode.
Do everything with joy,[3]
including facing this current challenge.

---

[1] Philippians 4:4; 1 Thessalonians 5:16.
[2] Romans 14:17; Hebrews 12:2; John 15:11.
[3] Deuteronomy 12:7,18.

April 6

Dear friend:

Here I am –

together with you in this place of feeling defeated.[1]

It's a good thing to recognize

when you are unable to do something.

There is no shame in this.

Actually, there is no toxic shame in this.

Instead, it is healthy shame to acknowledge limitations.[2]

One characteristic of good mental health

is to acknowledge that you are limited.

It's actually a very good place to be.

Where you are weak,

that is where I can be strong on your behalf.[3]

"Resist the devil, (my love,) and he will flee..."[4]

Do not tolerate the least bit of negativity.[5]

You are right that you are being harassed

for the purpose of distracting you from your work.

Be alert and watch for this.

In fact, watch for distractions from unexpected sources,

like when I discerned

Satan distracting me through Peter.[6]

---

[1] Matthew 28:20b.
[2] Matthew 5:3.
[3] 2 Corinthians 12:9-10.
[4] James 4:7b (NIV).
[5] Philippians 4:8; Romans 12:9.
[6] Matthew 16:21-23; Mark 8:31-33.

April 7

My treasure, my love:
Come to me, and I will give you rest.[1]
Lean on me and learn from me.[2]
You are busy disqualifying yourself.
Although you are in good company –
take Moses[3] or Gideon,[4] for example –
It will do no good.
What I have ordained, I have ordained.[5]
Do not resist this –
that will only make it less pleasant for you.
Surrender to my will[6] and experience this unfold as it must.
Embrace what I have placed in your heart[7] and run with it.
You may not know it all now,
But you will gradually live into it.
You may as well do it with joy,[8] my love.

---

[1] Matthew 11:28.
[2] Matthew 11:29.
[3] Exodus 3.
[4] Judges 6.
[5] Psalm 42:8; Psalm 32:8 (NLT); Philippians 2:13; Psalm 139:16.
[6] Romans 12:2; Ephesians 5:10; Colossians 1:9-10.
[7] Ephesians 2:10.
[8] Deuteronomy 12:7,18; Philippians 3:1.

April 8

My love:

Let's talk about how to deal with suffering.

It involves surrender and gratitude.

You are confusing surrendering with giving in. Giving in is weak resignation. Surrendering is a strong faith action. It was because Jesus fully surrendered to my will[1] that he was able to destroy the works of the enemy.[2] Combatting suffering begins with relinquishing your will and surrendering to mine. When you fully surrender to me, then you are in good shape to fight.

Determine to stay in a place of gratitude. Giving thanks in all things is not optional![3] As you stay surrendered to my will, you will be able to remain grateful. As you remain grateful, you will be able to stay surrendered to my will. In that place of surrender and gratitude, you will be able to discern how I want you to respond.

When you are resisting what is happening, you cannot hear my voice. When you resist suffering, you are asserting your will. Humble yourself before me. Then I will lift you up[4] and enable you to deal with suffering.

So: It's about surrender and gratitude and humility!

Of course, the main weapon in fighting Satan is love.[5] Do what love motivates you to do.[6] Do what you would want others to do for you.[7]

---

[1] John 5:30; John 6:38.
[2] 1 John 3:8.
[3] 1 Thessalonians 5:18; Ephesians 5:20.
[4] James 4:10; 1 Peter 5:6.
[5] 1 John 3:16.
[6] 1 Corinthians 13; Ephesians 5:2.
[7] Matthew 7:12.

April 9

My treasure, my love:
Do you know that no one has life apart from me?
There is no life or any being of any kind –
animate or inanimate –
apart from me.
I am the source of all life and I am Life.[1]
This is why it is unreasonable and nonsensical to not honor me.
This is why it is laughable
for a human being to look inside,
find my life,
and claim ownership of it.
No, my love – that is the height of folly and arrogance.
The truth is that all life emanates from me and is of me.
The only reasonable attitude
is that of gratitude,
humble worship,
and joyful surrender.

---

[1] John 1:4; John 5:26; John 11:25; John 14:6; 1 Corinthians 8:6.

April 10

My treasure, my love:
My joy is for you to experience right now.[1]
You do not need to wait
until every obstacle is removed
to be joyful.
My joy is not contingent on circumstances.
My joy emanates from who I am.
I am joyous!
I am joyful!
As my child, you too are joyous.
Do not take on the energy of negative circumstances.
You need to see yourself as separate from your circumstances.
Do not let your circumstances define who you are.
You are my child.[2]
You are deeply and unconditionally loved.[3]
You are created in my image.[4]
This means you live love because you are love.
You live joy because you are joy.
You live serenity because you are serenity.
You live gratitude because you are gratitude.
This reality of your being is deeper
than your thoughts and feelings.
Your thoughts and feelings must be reined in
and taught to submit
to who you are.

---

[1] John 15:9-11; Romans 14:17; Luke 17:21; Nehemiah 8:10.
[2] 1 John 3:1.
[3] Romans 5:8; 1 John 4:16.
[4] Genesis 1:27; Ephesians 4:24.

April 11

My treasure, my love:

I am your Shepherd.[1]

I am leading and guiding you.

I am placing my desires for you in your heart.[2]

I can't show you the big plan because it would scare you.

As you are faithful with what I give you,

I will give you more.[3]

Put your hope in me and do not be deterred.[4]

Do not be deterred by discouragement or fear.

Do not be hampered

by what has, or has not, happened in the past.

This is a new day.

Speak your desires,[5] put your hope in me, and wait.[6]

Wait for the fullness of time.[7]

Wait for my will to be revealed.[8]

Be faithful with what you have[9]

and watch for signs of what is to come.

Refuse to entertain discouragement or sadness.

My joy is your strength!

Let this be your mantra:

"The joy of the LORD is (my) strength."[10]

Let this truth be your mast, your sail, and your anchor.

---

[1] Psalm 23; John 10:11.

[2] Ezekiel 36:26; Psalm 51:10; Jeremiah 24:7; 2 Corinthians 5:17.

[3] Matthew 25:14-23.

[4] Psalm 42; Proverbs 3:5; 1 Peter 1:21.

[5] John 15:7; Philippians 4:6.

[6] Psalm 27:14; Micah 7:7; Romans 8:25.

[7] Galatians 4:4; Ephesians 1:10.

[8] Ephesians 5:17; Colossians 1:9.

[9] Matthew 25:14-30.

[10] Nehemiah 8:10d (NASB).

April 12

My treasure, my love:
In the stillness of the morning
it is easier for you to hear my voice.[1]
Draw close to me;[2] let my arms enfold you.
Rest your head on me and lean into me.
I know your pain;
I have made my home with you
and I feel this pain together with you.[3]
It is challenging to feel pain and still be at peace.
Resisting the source of the pain increases its intensity.
I have created you to be able to feel pain.
Feel it and then let it go.
You are not your feelings; you are not this pain.
In your spirit you are perfectly calm because there,
in the core of your being,
you know that everything is in my hands.[4]

---

[1] Psalm 143:8; Isaiah 50:4.
[2] Psalm 73:28; Hebrews 10:22; James 4:8a.
[3] John 14:23.
[4] Hebrews 1:3a; Colossians 1:16-17.

April 13

My treasure, my love:
If you check in your spirit –
the place where you and I commune[1] –
you will find peace and joy.
The challenge is to still and quiet your soul[2]
and to live from that place.
Your mind, will, and emotions
are tools that you use to serve.
But your spirit is your place of being.
It is a most beautiful place –
it shimmers with iridescent joy and peace and love.
It is a place of infinite possibilities.
It is the place from which you speak your purpose,
your truth,
and your creating words.

---

[1] John 14:23.
[2] Psalm 131:2; Psalm 62:1.

April 14

My treasure, my love:
..."I know the plans I have for you...
plans to prosper you and not to harm you,
plans to give you hope and a future."[1]
I am at work in you, my love,
causing you to will and to do my purpose.[2]
Everything is unfolding as it should.[3]
Your way will be made easier
as you surrender to my will
and make resisting a thing of the past.
Your way will be made easier
as you surrender to my will
and make striving a thing of the past.
You have prayed for my will to be done in your life
and I am answering that prayer.
There is no point in resisting or striving.
Replace resisting with gratitude.
Replace striving with rest.

---

[1] Jeremiah 29:11 (NIV).
[2] Philippians 2:13.
[3] Psalm 138:8 (NLT).

April 15

My treasure, my love:
Enter into my rest.[1]
Cease striving and enter into my rest.
I have completed the work
and you can walk in that completion.
The healings you seek already have happened.
They exist in my Yes! place.
Learn to live in that Yes! place.
It's the place of what is asked in my Name.[2]
It's the place of what is asked in accordance with my will.[3]
It's the place of what is asked that is motivated by love.[4]
It's the place of what is asked with an attitude of gratitude.[5]
And it's the place of what is asked with a believing heart.[6]
So enter into my rest.
Enter into my Yes! place.
Whatever you ask, see it as already accomplished.
See it as history.
And be grateful.[7]

---

[1] Hebrews 4:1-11; Matthew 11:28-30.
[2] John 14:13-14; John 15:16; John 16:23-24.
[3] Luke 22:42; Matthew 6:10.
[4] 1 Corinthians 13.
[5] Philippians 4:6.
[6] Mark 11:24.
[7] Hebrews 12:28.

April 16

My lovely one:
I invite you to place yourself and this situation
into my tender loving care.[1]
My intention is to use this experience
to bring good to you and to others.[2]
From my perspective, my love, all is well.
Nothing of this circumstance
changes the reality of your life being hidden in me[3]
and immersed in my love.[4]
Furthermore, nothing of this circumstance
changes the reality of my life being hidden in you![5]
The judgments of human beings –
including your own –
do not alter this reality.
It is time for you to take yourself and others
off of my judgment throne.
None of you are in a position to judge you.
I insist on this –
look at the great grief it is causing you!
It is robbing you of peace, of joy, and of the desire to live.
It is time for a new beginning, my love.
Leave the past in the past and move on.

---

[1] 1 Peter 5:7; Psalm 55:22.
[2] Romans 8:28
[3] Colossians 3:3.
[4] Romans 8:38-39.
[5] John 14:23; John 17:23; Romans 8:10; Galatians 2:20; Ephesians 3:16-17.

April 17

My love:

Pay no attention to that old condemning voice.[1]

Step out of that old way of striving for perfection.

I have no need for you to perform flawlessly.[2]

Your new life, my life in you,

has no need for you to make no mistakes.

We adore you just as you are.[3]

In fact, your new life, the life of Christ,

is holy and blameless, without a single fault.[4]

So walk in that reality – be set free in that truth.[5]

Another thing: you do not need

unconditional love and acceptance from others

to be able to feel good about yourself.

They are not your source. I am your source.[6]

You came from me,[7]

you live in me,[8]

and you will return to me[9] –

other people's opinions of you

are totally irrelevant to this reality.

Their evaluation of you must remain exterior to your life.

---

[1] Romans 8:1; Romans 8:34; Ephesians 4:20-24.
[2] Hebrews 4:15-16.
[3] Romans 5:8.
[4] Colossians 1:22 (NLT); Ephesians 1:4.
[5] John 8:32.
[6] Job 33:4; Psalm 16:2.
[7] Psalm 119:73; Psalm 139:13.
[8] John 15:4: 1 John 4:15.
[9] John 14:3.

April 18

My treasure:
I alone am your Judge.[1]
Do not bow to the judgment of anyone or anything else.
To do so is to worship a false god.
Look at the fruit of this idol worship:
condemnation and shame,
demoralization and despair.
No! Do not do this!
I alone am your God![2]
I alone am your Judge.

---

[1] John 5:22; John 5:27.
[2] Exodus 20:3; Matthew 4:10.

April 19

The solution for guilt, my love, is to confess your sin
and receive my forgiveness and cleansing.[1]
There is no need to stay under the burden of guilt
for one second beyond recognition of sin.
You have confessed your sin;
receive my forgiveness and cleansing.
Imagine a giant-sized eraser
erasing all the sin and guilt from your past.
From my perspective, all your misdeeds are gone.
Erased. Wiped out. Vanished.[2]
As for the shame:
You would not be feeling shame
if you were not concerned
about what others might be thinking.
You are giving others permission to judge you.
The solution for shame
is to get these people off my throne!
I alone am able to judge.[3]
Stand in what you know to be true
and give no thought to what others might be thinking.
So, take another eraser
and erase what you think others might be thinking.
Then take another eraser
and erase everything anyone said that was not true.
Only what is true will endure to the end.[4]
My love, you can stand tall and strong because of who I am
and because of what I have done for you on the cross.[5]
There is no guilt or shame for those who are in Christ Jesus.[6]

---

[1] 1 John 1:9.
[2] Psalm 103:12; Isaiah 43:25; Acts 3:19.
[3] John 5:22; John 5:27; John 5:30.
[4] Proverbs 12:19; Matthew 24:35; John 14:6.
[5] Colossians 1:20.
[6] Romans 8:1; Colossians 1:22.

April 20

My love, my treasure:
I was there when you were born.[1]
I want you to know
that there was great rejoicing in heaven on that day!
Yes! It was a day of great celebration!
All of my court knew the importance of your birth.
It was not an inconsequential thing, your birth.
Your parents may have wanted a child different from you;
I, however, wanted you!
It was more important for my purposes
that you were born.
You were exactly the person I wanted.
You were perfect in every way.
I would not change one thing about you, my love.
You are exactly as I desire.[2]
Make no mistake – you are just as I want you to be.
I am fully pleased with you, just as you are.
When you were born, I sang a happy song over you.[3]
And I still am singing happy songs over you!
So put aside any worries
about the opinions of any human beings.
Put aside any concerns about not being wanted.
Your origin and your destiny are in my heart.[4]
Your challenge is to live your life
knowing your place in my heart.
That was the secret of my Son—

---

[1] Psalm 139.
[2] Genesis 1:31.
[3] Zephaniah 3:17.
[4] Ephesians 2:10.

He knew his place in my heart.[1]
You can know it too, my love.
And so, that's how it began.
And that's how it will end –
with me singing a happy song over you
as you come to enjoy the place I have prepared for you![2]

---

[1] John 1:18 (NLT).
[2] John 14:3.

April 21

My treasure, my love:
You are in a very good place.
It is a good thing to be stripped of everything.[1]
Jesus was stripped of everything.
He became nothing - a helpless human being.
And when he found himself in that stripped position,
He chose to surrender every aspect of his life
in complete trust and obedience.[2]
The beauty of being stripped
and of knowing that you are stripped, my love,
is that you then are free to surrender.

---

[1] Matthew 5:3.
[2] Philippians 2:5-11.

April 22

My treasure, my love:
The fear you experience is not who you are.
Fear is just a feeling I created to help you live.
It is the normal, healthy response to danger.
It is what motivates you to stay away from danger.
The reason you do not need to be afraid
is because I am with you.[1]
It's not that there is no danger –
Bad things can happen at any time.
However, I am holding you in the palm of my hand.[2]
That's why you can relax and be serene.
The way to cope with danger is to stay in me.[3]
Sometimes you feel fear
because you are remembering times
when you experienced danger.
Sometimes you feel fear
because you are fantasizing danger in the future.
Danger in the past cannot harm you – it no longer exists.
Danger in the future cannot harm you –
it does not exist either.
You have only this moment
in which I am keeping you safe.[4]
I repeat: You are not the fear you experience.
You are my child – my dearly loved child.[5]
Because I am love,[6] you are love.
Celebrate this love and be happy.

---

[1] Isaiah 41:10; Isaiah 43:1-3; Matthew 28:20b.
[2] Isaiah 49:2; Isaiah 51:16; Isaiah 62:3.
[3] John 15:4; Colossians 2:6.
[4] Psalm 91.
[5] 1 John 3:1; John 1:12; Romans 8:16.
[6] 1 John 4:16.

April 23

My treasure, my love:
Whether you are happy or sad,
Whether you are energetic or lethargic,
Whether you accomplish
a miniscule or a phenomenal amount,
My love for you
and my appreciation of you
remains constant.[1]
Actually, it is over the moon.
My love for you is enormous.
It is incalculable.[2]
And it is near –
you are enveloped in it and infused by it.[3]
Celebrate my love for you and be very glad!

---

[1] Zephaniah 3:17.
[2] Psalm 36:5 (NLT); Psalm103:11 (NLT); Ephesians 3:18-19.
[3] 1 John 4:16.

April 24

My treasure, my love:
You have come to a parting of the ways.
One way has seemed like a way,
but it has become so unclear
that it is no longer distinguishable.
The other way is shouting out to you
but you have not heard
because of your adherence to the former way.
You have become lost
because you have been attending to the former way.
Listen for the other way.
You will find that I am there, too.[1]
You will find that it is a way of peace and joy.[2]
You will find that it is a way
of effortless purpose and fulfillment.
We will take all that you are and have
and craft it into a new way of being and doing.[3]
Get your hopes up, my love.[4]
Get your hopes up and be very glad!
I am your God;[5] I am your Shepherd,[6]
And I am leading you in the perfect path for you.[7]

[1] Psalm 139:7-12.
[2] Romans 14:17; Romans 15:13.
[3] Isaiah 64:8.
[4] 1 Peter 1:13; Romans 4:18; Romans 15:13.
[5] Ezekiel 34:31; Isaiah 41:10.
[6] Psalm 23; John 10:11.
[7] Psalm 32:8 (NLT).

April 25

My treasure, my love:

I love it that you try to listen to the still, small voice of my Spirit![1]

I love it that you are facing and expressing the anger you feel about what has happened in your life.

I know about your anger.

I also know about the pain underneath the anger.

Those wounds need to be lanced and cleansed.

When we meet face-to-face I will tell you about everything that was accomplished in your every endeavor.

Now I ask you, if the Apostle Paul had kept coming to me with regrets about his former activities to persecute Christians,[2] what would have been accomplished? He needed to surrender to my having allowed that to happen. He needed to trust that I was bringing good out of that.[3] He needed to let that go so he could receive my instructions for each day.

In the same way, you need to surrender to what I have allowed and to what I have ordained. Until you have let go of all your anger and regret and disappointment and shame and guilt about the past, it will be difficult for you to receive my mandate for your future.

Choose to surrender to my will and my way regarding the past so you can embrace my will and my way regarding your future.

---

[1] 1 Kings 19:11-13.
[2] Acts 9. (This Saul became the Apostle Paul – see Acts 13:9.)
[3] Romans 8:28.

April 26

My treasure, my love:
Why are you so downcast?
What lie are you believing that is creating this despair?
The truth, my love, is that you are blessed immeasurably.
If you could see the truth of your existence,[1]
you would laugh.
Yes, you would laugh!
Feeling shame and despair is an old habit.
It is old and worn out – like a tattered trench coat.
You need to take it off
and put on a new, beautiful coat of joy.[2]
You've done your time in the trenches.
Get out of there and throw off that ragged coat!
Lift your face to the sun of my smile[3] and laugh.
Put on your multi-colored coat of iridescent joy and laugh.
Laugh to your good health!

[1] Ephesians 1:18-21.
[2] Colossians 3:9-10; Romans 13:14; John 15:11.
[3] Numbers 6:24-26; Psalm 67:1.

April 27

My treasure, my love:
There is a battle going on in your soul:
Are you going to rest in me or continue to strive?
Are you going to trust that I will provide
or continue to struggle?
That was the battle taking place
when Jacob wrestled with the "man."[1]
Jacob's striving was very strong –
it could not be overcome by human strength.
He had to discover that he was struggling with me.
So the "man" touched his hip,
putting it out of joint
and leaving Jacob with a limp.
Jacob was afraid
because he didn't realize
that his destiny was in my hands.
He thought his struggle was with human beings –
with his uncle and with his brother –
but it was with me.
You can learn from this.
You are afraid
because you don't realize
that your destiny is in my hands.
You think your struggle is with people, but it is with me.
Your challenge is to believe
that your destiny is in my hands.
The "man" put Jacob's hip out of joint
to show him that he was struggling with me.

---

[1] Genesis 32.

When Jacob realized he was wrestling with me,
that his destiny was in my hands,
then He asked me for a blessing
and I gave him a new name.
The new name signified a change
in his identity and way of being.
No longer would he be
the one who struggles with humans to prevail.
Instead, he would be
the one who struggles with God and prevails.
No longer would he be
the one who relies on his own strength
to control his destiny.
Instead, he would be
the one who relies on God to determine his destiny.
You can choose to trust me to provide,
or continue to be afraid.

April 28

My treasure, my love:
Be still and know my love for you.[1]
Bask in my love for you.
Immerse yourself in my limitless love.[2]
I am your Shepherd and I am all you need.[3]
You are clamoring for approval from people.
This is a false god.
Like all false gods, it will prove to be fickle.
Instead of looking to people for approval,
look to me.[4]
It is my approval you really need.
I give you my limitless, unconditional approval!
I approve of you, my love!
I adore you just as you are.
I delight in you.[5]
Let my approval be the foundation for your life.
Build your hope and your identity
on my joy and delight in you.
Choose to be grateful
for opportunities to withstand
the temptation to find approval in people.
Every time someone rejects what you have to offer,
see it as a reminder to celebrate my approval of you.

---

[1] Ephesians 3:16-19.
[2] Psalm 36:5; Psalm 103:11.
[3] Psalm 23:1; 2 Corinthians 9:8.
[4] Proverbs 29:25; Matthew 22:16.
[5] Zephaniah 3:17 (NLT).

April 29

My treasure, my love:
Let me hold you close to my heart.[1]
Do you know how special this is?
Do you know that this oneness we enjoy[2]
is the most precious experience
a human being can have?
Truly, my love, it doesn't get better than this!
So just enjoy it. Savor it. Relish it!
Go back to it again and again.
Do you know that you can enjoy this intimacy
in absolutely any circumstance?

---

[1] Psalm 91:4.
[2] John 14:23; John 17:20-23; Revelation 3:20.

April 30

My treasure, my love:
Faith is being sure of what you hope for.[1]
It is being certain of what you do not see.
Faith is putting your eyes on me.[2]
It is resting on my promises.[3]
Faith is what makes life exciting!
It's going to be fun for you to see how I provide.
And you can be certain that I will provide![4]

---

[1] Hebrews 11:1.
[2] Hebrews 12:2.
[3] 2 Corinthians 1:20.
[4] Philippians 4:19.

May

May 1

My treasure, my love:
You do not need to be perfect
in your ability to hear my voice.
It's okay to make mistakes.
It's not okay to give up!
I love your determination –
It's one of my favorite things about you!
Keep living your life with zest.[1]
Don't worry about going in the wrong direction.
You can count on me to provide a course correction.[2]
It's true that sometimes you "hear" me
saying things I am not saying.
I'm not upset about that.
I know that eventually you'll get it right.
The beautiful thing is that you are reaching out to me.[3]
There is life in that interaction
even if the details sometimes are flawed.
So let's just continue this journey together through life.
You and me.
Hand in hand.[4]
Arm in arm.
Heart in heart.[5]
I love you, my precious child![6]

---

[1] Colossians 3:23.
[2] Psalm 32:8 (NLT); Psalm 73:23-24; Matthew 11:29.
[3] Psalm 27:8; Psalm 105:3-4; Isaiah 55:6.
[4] Psalm 73:23; John 14:23.
[5] Ezekiel 36:26-27; Joel 2:29; 1 Corinthians 3:16.
[6] 1 John 3:1.

May 2

My treasure, my love:
Even though you feel lost, you're not.
Even though you think you don't know the way, you do.
Even though you think you're giving up
something extremely valuable,
You simply are making room
for something just as valuable.
Walk confidently into the future, my love!
I have such joy planned for you![1]
Embrace this time of change and the change itself.
Know that I surround you[2] and I go before you.[3]
I fill you[4] and I energize you.[5]
It's you and me together,
sashaying boldly into the future.
You'll see!
What joy!
Pure, unadulterated joy!
You and me together.
Yes. I like it!!

---

[1] Jeremiah 29:11; Isaiah 55:12; Romans 15:13.
[2] Psalm 3:3; Psalm 34:7.
[3] Deuteronomy 31:8.
[4] Ephesians 5:18.
[5] Isaiah 40:31.

May 3

My treasure, my love:
Still and quiet your soul in my presence.[1]
My treasure, you and I go back a long ways.
We have history that can never be erased.
There may be misunderstandings,
there may be unresolved issues,
but our relationship is rock solid.
There may be times when you doubt me –
when you are tempted to question my Word[2] –
But my Word has been planted
deep in the soil of your heart and it is bearing fruit.[3]
It is bearing the fruit of righteousness.[4]
Lately you have looked back at your life.
You have seen the struggle and you have been discouraged.
I would like to tell you that you are not in a position
to assess what happened.
You do not have adequate information
to make a judgment.
My intention is to redeem everything.[5]
I encourage you to look to the future rather than the past.
I am giving you a hope and a future so look to the future.[6]
My treasure, my love,
Put your hope in me.[7]
Rest in me.[8]
Find your peace and joy in me.[9]

---

[1] Psalm 131:2; Psalm 62:1.
[2] Genesis 3:1.
[3] Mark 4:20.
[4] Philippians 1:9-11.
[5] Romans 8:28.
[6] Jeremiah 29:11.
[7] Psalm 42:5; Psalm 31:24; 1 Peter 1:21.
[8] Matthew 11:28-29.
[9] Romans 15:13.

May 4

My treasure, my love:
I am faithfully completing the work I began in you.[1]
You will soon see, my love, that you have nothing to fear.
I am your mighty Savior[2]
and I am looking after everything for you.
Rest in me – my grace is sufficient for you.[3]
These things you find unacceptable are not unacceptable.
Instead, they are exactly what is needed.
You are right to embrace them.
You are wise to embrace them!
Mostly, they are very interesting.
Be curious about them and about what I am doing.
You can be assured that I am doing something!
I'm always doing something and it's something good.
Just remember:
My plans are for good and not for disaster.[4]
So you can relax.
Relax and rejoice.[5]
And be grateful.[6]

---

[1] Philippians 1:6.
[2] Zephaniah 3:17 (NLT).
[3] 2 Corinthians 12:9.
[4] Jeremiah 29:11.
[5] Philippians 4:4.
[6] Colossians 3:15.

May 5

Beautiful treasure:
You can relax today, knowing that you are enough.
I am not asking anything more of you
than you gave today.
Actually, it was more than enough!
You did so many things for so many people today.
I want to thank you,
because in serving others,
you served me.[1]
Thank you, my dear friend!

---

[1] Matthew 25:40.

May 6

My treasure, my love:
I am the Lord of all.[1]
This had to happen.
You know that sometimes bad things have to happen
before good things can take place.
Do you remember the wild blueberry patches
that get burned in fall for fruit in spring?
You can leave these ones you love more than life
in my tender care.[2]
My promise to you is that you will enjoy eternity
together with them.[3]
So let them go.
They will travel some rocky roads to get there,
but get there they will![4]
You can take the stance
of a caring and interested bystander,
watching to see what I do in their lives.
Love them and let them go.
My treasure, my love:
It is possible for you to experience peace and joy
no matter what is happening in their lives.
Their lives are quite separate from yours.
Do you remember what I said to Peter
when he asked me about John?[5]
I will say the same to you: If I want this or that for these ones you
love, that is not your concern. Your focus is to follow me.
Yes, follow me.
You will find great joy and peace in simply following me.[1]

---

[1] Acts 10:36; Matthew 28:18; Hebrews 1:3a.
[2] Psalm 36:7; Psalm 40:5.
[3] Titus 1:2 (NLT); 1 John 2:25.
[4] Matthew 18:12-14; 2 Peter 3:9.
[5] John 21:20-22.

May 7

My treasure, my love:
Move in really close to me.[2]
Let me hold you tight while you do this rant
about everything that is so unacceptable to you!
Remember that your destiny already is written.[3]
Yes it is.
And it's characterized by joy,[4] my love.
So accept and love
everything that I am giving you
day by day.
Love it all!
And choose to do more of what gives you joy.
Choose to do what you think might give you joy.

---

[1] Romans 15:13.
[2] John 15:1-17
[3] Psalm 139:16.
[4] John 15:11.

May 8

My treasure, my love:
When the time is right...
For some people, any time is the right time.
And maybe for them it really doesn't matter.
In my Kingdom, however, timing is critical.[1]
I've got everything planned down to the nanosecond.[2]
It's so much fun to work out to a split second
all the details in the lives of my friends!
The neat thing is that I can do that
without interfering with their free will –
Now that's what it is to be all-powerful!
I would love for you to truly understand this.
Then you would relax about everything.
You would just know that I've got it all in hand.[3]
My treasure, my love – I've got it all in hand!

---

[1] John 7:6 (NLT).
[2] Psalm 138:8 (NLT); Isaiah 46:9-10; Ephesians 1:11.
[3] Hebrews 1:3a; Colossians 1:16-17.

May 9

My treasure, my love:
Be assured that I am present with you in this place of pain.[1]
I invite you to take this entire grief and lay it on my cross.
Take this sorrow –
past, present, and future –
and lay it on the cross.
I have borne this for you.[2]
You are right that it is too intense for you to bear.
That is why I carried it for you.
So gather up this sorrow –
past, present, and future –
and put it in a basket.
Take this basket to my cross and leave it there.
My treasure, my love:
My intention is for you to experience peace and joy.[3]
I paid the supreme price
for you to be able to enter my rest.[4]
I have accomplished this for you –
receive my gift of grace.[5]

---

[1] Matthew 28:20b.
[2] Isaiah 53:4.
[3] Romans 14:17; Romans 15:13.
[4] Hebrews 4:1-11; Matthew 11:28-30.
[5] John 1:16.

May 10

My treasure, my lovely one:
I constantly look for faith[1] and I reward faith.[2]
"Without faith it is impossible to please (me)."[3]
With faith, all things are possible.[4]
I know your grief and I am with you in your grief.
However, I do not reward grief.
It is not grief that moves mountains.
It is not begging that moves mountains.
It is not even worship that moves mountains.
It is faith that moves mountains.[5]
Faith comes by getting to know me.
The Syrophoenician woman[6] was certain
that I could give her what she needed.
So she pressed in until I met her request.
She would not be dissuaded.
She focused on my power and my love.
She knew that I could give her what she needed
and she pressed in until love constrained a response.
Faith in me moves mountains.

---

[1] Luke 18:8b.
[2] Mark 5:24b-34; Matthew 8:5-13.
[3] Hebrews 11:6a (NIV).
[4] Mark 9:23.
[5] Mark 11:23.
[6] Mark 7:24-30.

May 11

My treasure, my precious one:
I am living in and through you.[1]
I am so very pleased to live in and through you!
I am a spring of living water welling up inside you.[2]
This is a very deep spring of pure, sweet water.
Others draw from this water
without you even knowing it.
You are yoked with me and it is an easy yoke
because I do it all.[3]
So just relax.
Enter into my rest[4] and enjoy the ride.

---

[1] John 17:20-23; Galatians 2:20; Romans 8:10.
[2] John 4:14.
[3] Matthew 11:29-30.
[4] Hebrews 4:1-11; Matthew 11:28-30.

May 12

My treasure:
The pursuit of happiness is not advised.
Happiness is one of the fruits of a life of obedience.
Make obedience your aim[1] –
especially my command to love.[2]
Stated succinctly: Make love your aim.[3]

---

[1] Galatians 5:13-26.
[2] John 15:9-17.
[3] 2 John 1:6.

May 13

My love, my treasure:
Lift up your head and be glad,[1] child of mine![2]
Let all your worries flow into the river of my love
and be lost forever.
I am going ahead of you and preparing the way for you[3] –
Worry is fundamentally illogical
and so ludicrous as to be laughable!
More than anyone else on the face of the earth,
those who know they are my children
can throw back their heads and laugh.
They can afford to be carefree
and to enjoy every good thing
I am providing minute by minute.[4]
Living in a place of joy and gratitude
is fundamentally logical, my love.
When you are not in that place,
you are out of touch with reality.
Choose to be in that place of joy and gratitude
every minute of every day,
for that is where I am
and that is where I desire you to be.
It is the place I have prepared for you –
A place of joy and gratitude and love.
The other things that are happening
are secondary and transitory.
Celebrate joy and gratitude and love
today and tomorrow and tomorrow....

---

[1] Psalm 32:11; Philippians 4:4.
[2] John 1:12; 1 John 3:1.
[3] Deuteronomy 31:8; Ephesians 1:11.
[4] James 1:17; Philippians 4:19.

May 14

My treasure, my love:
Embrace the future I have planned for you.[1]
I am moving you into a time of fruitfulness.
Follow your heart and the leading of my Spirit.
Don't bother trying to orchestrate anything –
I've got it all in hand.[2]
Seriously! I am looking after every detail.
The intricacies of what I am doing
would make your head spin!
So don't bother trying to control things.
And don't bother trying to figure things out.
Just do what I motivate you to do each day[3]
and all will be well.
Afterwards, you will be able to see
the beautiful unfolding of my plan.
I love this –
this working out my purposes
in the lives of my children.[4]
It gives me great joy!
So just let me look after things
while you have fun doing what I cause you to do.
I love you, my treasure.

---

[1] Jeremiah 29:11.
[2] Hebrews 1:3a; Colossians 1:16-17.
[3] Philippians 2:13.
[4] Psalm 138:8 (NLT); Ephesians 1:11; Isaiah 46:9-10.

May 15

My treasure, my love:
Even though you are very apprehensive
about heading in a new direction,
you will be courageous and follow where I am leading.
And be assured that I am charting this course![1]
Throw back your head
and laugh in the face of the unknown,
because wherever you go,
I am there with you.[2]
Turn every concern into a prayer request[3]
and believe that you have received it.[4]
Make your prayer requests big enough to honor me.
Remember—you are deeply and unconditionally loved.[5]
Let's go on this journey together,
enjoying each other every step of the way!

---

[1] Psalm 37:23
[2] Matthew 28:20b.
[3] Philippians 4:6.
[4] Mark 11:24.
[5] Psalm 36:5,7; Psalm 103:11; Ephesians 3:17-19.

May 16

My child, my dearly loved child:
It is a difficult thing
to face the depravity in the human heart.[1]
It is especially difficult
to recognize that depravity in your own soul.
Seeing it, acknowledging it, and owning it
are necessary first steps to addressing it.
When you see and acknowledge and own this depravity,
then you know your need for a Savior.[2]
That's when you have attained the poverty in spirit
that is a prerequisite for receiving my gift of grace.[3]
Awareness of depravity is not a bad thing.
In fact, it's a very good thing that is essential to salvation.
When you recognize that depravity within yourself,
don't turn away from me
and give in to despair and self-condemnation.
Instead, run towards my embrace
and celebrate once more the righteousness, peace, and joy
that you have in Christ Jesus.[4]
My forgiveness is perpetual and endless.[5]
My love is unconditional.
Only those who know their need
can receive my love and forgiveness.
Blessed are those who know their need for God,
for the Kingdom of Heaven is given to them.[6]

---

[1] Jeremiah 17:9; Mark 7:21-23.
[2] Mark 2:16-17.
[3] Matthew 5:3.
[4] Romans 14:17.
[5] 1 John 1:9.
[6] Matthew 5:3.

May 17

My treasure, my love:
Today I would like to talk to you about miracles.
My thoughts are not quite the same
as your thoughts[1] on miracles.
In one sense,
everything that happens on earth is a miracle
because nothing is possible in this realm
apart from my energizing, imbuing presence.[2]
On the other hand,
nothing is miraculous
because nothing is impossible with me.[3]
As you grow in your experience of intimacy with me,
you will quit finding it challenging
to believe for out-of-the-ordinary happenings
and you will quit being surprised by these "miracles."
Ten years from now,
when you have matured in this regard,
you'll look back and say,
"I remember God talking to me about this…"
I'm enjoying being together with you
in this place of gratitude and joy.
My face is shining with a beautiful smile
as I look at you, my love.[4]
My mercies are new every day
and my faithfulness is completely reliable.[5]

---

[1] Isaiah 55:9.
[2] Hebrews 1:3a; Colossians 1:16-17.
[3] Mark 10:27; Jeremiah 32:17.
[4] Numbers 6:24-26; Psalm 67:1.
[5] Lamentations 3:22-23.

May 18

My treasure, my love:
There is no need to be troubled about this issue.
I am quite capable of working this out for you.[1]
Be assured that I am present with you
as you struggle through this.[2]
You are right about the priority of obedience.
You also are right about the importance of letting go.
Letting go involves surrendering –
surrendering your will to mine.[3]
Abraham had to be ready to let go of Isaac.[4]
In the same way,
you need to be ready to let go of everything.
When you think that something must be thus and so,
then I will ask you to let it go.
The perfectly surrendered will
makes no declarations about what must be.
Remember that I am at work in you,
causing you to will and to do my purpose.[5]
Still and quiet your soul to discern my will.[6]
You will find that my will
is in the center of what you desire.
I cause you to will, to desire to do my purpose.
Leave your loved ones in my tender loving care.[7]

---

[1] Philippians 4:6-7.
[2] Isaiah 41:10; Isaiah 43:2; Matthew 28:20b.
[3] Luke 22:42; Matthew 6:10.
[4] Genesis 22:1-18.
[5] Philippians 2:13.
[6] Psalm 131:2; Psalm 62:5; Psalm 130:5.
[7] Matthew 6:25-34.

You can rest assured that I will complete the good work
that I have begun in each one of them.[1]
My treasure,
you can return to that place of joy and gratitude and love.
Let's resume our delight in each other in that place.
All is well, my love.
I am the God who created the ever-expanding universe
and I am causing all things
to unfold according to my plan.[2]

---

[1] Philippians 1:6.
[2] Psalm 138:8 (NLT); Ephesians 1:11; Isaiah 46:9-10.

May 19

My child:
You are asking me why you are not able to be sure
that I will cause you to walk in the way you should go.
I will tell you:
You are not completely trusting me
to manage my business affairs.
You are looking
for certain things to happen at certain times
when this is my concern, not yours.
Yours is to be obedient each step of the way
and to leave results entirely up to me.
You have placed yourself in my hands so relax!
I will move you as I choose –
as I have in fact already been doing.[1]
And remember:
My way is to free you to do something,
not to drive you to do it out of fear or guilt.

---

[1] Philippians 2:13: Psalm 138:8 (NLT).

May 20

My treasure,
here we are again in that sacred place
where it's just the two of us.
How I love this place!
This is where we get to share with each other
what's in our hearts.
I'm glad you're not satisfied
because then you might not come to this place!
It's okay to not be satisfied.
What's not okay is to judge your experience as inadequate.
Instead of being inadequate, your experience is perfect.
It's perfect because it's just how I want it to be.
The time has come for you to stop judging your experience
and finding it inadequate.
Your life is unfolding according to my plan.[1]
If I wanted it to be different, I would make it so.
I am not looking at you, shaking my head,
and judging your life as inadequate!
You have no idea what is going on
behind the "seens" as your life unfolds.
One day you will know and understand.
For now just know that you have our approval.[2]
Extend that same approval to yourself and be content.
The glass is not half empty, my love, it's completely full!
Take that to the bank and cash it – you are loaded!!
There, I've given you the truth on the matter,
just as you asked.

---

[1] Psalm 138:8 (NLT); Ephesians 1:11; Isaiah 46:9-10.
[2] Zephaniah 3:17.

May 21

My love, draw close to me.[1] Let my strong arms enfold you. Lean your head on my shoulder.

I hold before me all the prayers you have ever prayed.[2] The truth is that I have responded to all of them. You have not yet lived into all the answers.

Continue to bring to me all your desires.[3] When you see something that is not as you would have it, look at that area with excitement and make your request with joyful anticipation of my creative response.[4]

Don't worry about how impossible something seems. Am I not the God of the impossible?[5] Do I not create something out of nothing?[6]

Of course, you will have to be patient because some requests require a time of brooding. See your requests as eggs and me as a mother hen brooding over that nest full of eggs.

I have not forgotten even one of your many prayers. My nest can hold as many prayers as you can pray and I delight in brooding over each one.

---

[1] James 4:8a.
[2] Psalm 10:17; Psalm 34:15; Psalm 145:19; 1 John 5:14-15.
[3] Psalm 37:4; Psalm 145:19.
[4] Philippians 4:6.
[5] Mark 10:27; Jeremiah 32:17.
[6] Hebrews 11:3.

May 22

Draw near to me, my love,
and listen to what my Spirit is saying in your spirit.[1]
My Spirit takes what is in my heart
and shares it with you.[2]
You are having a very difficult time
listening to my voice these days.
This is because you are experiencing the fruit of doubt.
Doubt will rob you and paralyze you.

---

[1] Proverbs 1:23; James 4:8a; Hebrews 10:22; John 16:13.
[2] John 16:14-15.

May 23

My love, my treasure:
I see you sitting there at my feet, waiting to hear me speak.
I see your efforts to clear your mind of distractions and your
patience.
You will not be disappointed!
I cherish these times when you choose "the better thing."[1]
I love to speak to you through my Word, through my other
children, through circumstances, through nature and all the other
ways I communicate.
To sit at my feet and listen in your spirit for words from my Spirit
is one of those ways.
It is a way that requires great courage and discipline.
I have created within you the desire for this communication and I
give you the courage and discipline to actually sit down and listen.

And with that lengthy preamble, I will say what I want to say to
you today.
Most importantly, I will never tire of telling you how much I love
you, my dearest friend![2]

And now: I want you to know that I am delighted with your
prayers for my son.[3]
I have not forgotten why I created him.
I have not forgotten my plan for his life.[4]
When the time is right, I look for intercessors to partner with me
in the work of speaking into existence my plans.

---

[1] Luke 10:38-42.
[2] John 15:14-15.
[3] Proverbs 15:8b.
[4] Psalm 138:8 (NLT).

That's why you are taking up this cause at this time.
Keep speaking what you believe to be true for him.
Speak the words you are given by my Spirit.[1]
Together we will speak into existence my plan for his life.
You don't have to argue with me
or convince me of this plan.
Instead, my desire is that you partner with me
in creating this plan, in calling it into being.
See it. Believe it. Articulate it. Celebrate it.
Never underestimate the power of your words.
I have created you in my image[2]
and that includes having the power
to speak things into existence.
You are many things to me:
my child, my treasure, my friend…
Today I am calling you to be my co-creator.
I want you to have fun with this!
Don't be afraid to use your imagination
and to say whatever you see.
I'll sort through it all and refine it
to perfectly suit my purposes.

---

[1] Romans 8:26-27; Titus 3:6.
[2] Genesis 1:27.

May 24

My love, come sit with me
and let's take a look at this experience.
No one knows more than I do
what a challenge this was for you!
You yielded yourself to the leading of my Spirit[1]
and we did it together.
From your perspective,
it was something you wanted to do and you did it.
From my perspective,
it was something I put in your heart
and motivated you to do.[2]
My love, you can't know how lives were transformed
and the positive ripple effect on many others,
but I see it clearly –
it is beautiful beyond description.
Your reward is surely in my hand,[3] my treasure!

---

[1] Galatians 5:25; Matthew 11:28-29.
[2] Philippians 2:13.
[3] Isaiah 49:4; Revelation 22:12.

May 25

My treasure, my love:
You are second-guessing the decisions you made in years past.
This is the same as second-guessing
my ability to lead and guide you.
You need have no regrets about the choices you made
because I was at work in and through you
and the circumstances in your life,
causing my will to be done.[1]
In the same way, I now am at work in your life.
The process of looking back
and seeing how I caused your life to unfold
can give you the confidence to know
that I am continuing to ensure
that you walk in the best path for your life.[2]
I want to remind you that it is not possible for you
to accurately assess the fruit of your obedience.
I place a high value even on those experiences
where the results of your decisions
seem to be characterized by a lack of success
or even seem undesirable.
Rest assured that your reward is in my hands.[3]
"There is…no condemnation for those who are in Christ Jesus."[4]
What can be different in your experience now
is the extent to which you relax and trust
that I am shepherding you
on this part of your journey through life.
Continue to seek me
and then simply do what you feel like doing –
I've got you covered!

---

[1] Philippians 2:13.
[2] Psalm 32:8 (NLT).
[3] Isaiah 49:4; Revelation 22:12.
[4] Romans 8:1 (ESV).

May 26

My precious treasure:

The things of earth seem so much more real than the things of the spirit.

The fact of the matter is, however, that the things of earth are mere shadows of the real.[1]

It is when you are communing with me that you are connecting with what is unmovable, unshakeable, permanent, and of true significance.

People live as though the things of earth have lasting value until they face the transition from life on earth to the next life.

Then they turn their attention to things in the world of the spirit.

How much better to have connected with the things of eternity long before that final passage!

How much better to have practiced hearing my voice long before you hear me calling you to your eternal home!

How much better to have gotten to know me well long before spending eternity with me![2]

You are wondering again about the many prayers you have prayed for which you have not yet received an affirmative response. What I want to say to you about that today is that for you to continue praying requires maturity. One day you will see what I have done with each one of your prayers. Until then, keep praying![3]

And keep laughing! Enjoy everything I provide for you each day,[4] my treasure, my love.

---

[1] Colossians 2:17.
[2] Jude 1:21.
[3] Luke 18:1-8; 1 Thessalonians 5:17.
[4] 1 Timothy 6:17.

May 27

Dear friend:
I see the concern you are experiencing
regarding this one you love.
It is the concern one experiences
when it seems that there are signs that all is not well.
The life experience of another is one of those things
that are "too wonderful" for you –
beyond your ability to understand and manage.[1]
So do not trouble yourself with it.
Keep your eyes fixed on me.[2]
Put your hope and confidence in my love
and in my ability to complete the work I have begun[3]
in this one you love.

---

[1] Psalm 131:1 (NIV).
[2] Psalm 141:8; Hebrews 12:2; Hebrews 3:1.
[3] Philippians 1:6.

May 28

My love, my treasure, my friend:
Let's just take this moment to enjoy our oneness.
You in me; I in you.[1]
I wouldn't have it any other way.
I always am everything you need, my love.[2]
With me inside you,
and you inside me,
you never lack anything!
So enjoy your position of wealth, my treasure.
I am blessing you
and together we bless the world.
Open your hands and heart
to receive all that I am giving you.
See yourself as a conduit of blessing,[3]
my treasure, my love, my friend.

---

[1] 1 John 4:15; John 14:23; John 17:20-23; Revelation 3:20.
[2] 2 Corinthians 9:8; Ephesians 3:20.
[3] John 7:38.

May 29

My precious friend:
I am delighted to take this burden from you.[1]
It is good to acknowledge wrongdoing
and to feel the associated guilt and shame,
but it is not my will for you to get stuck in the shame.
It was for those very misdeeds and that very shame
that I suffered and died.[2]
My desire for you
is that you experience freedom from guilt and shame[3]
so that you can live a life of peace and joy.[4]

---

[1] 1 John 1:9.
[2] Isaiah 53:5.
[3] Romans 8:33-34; 1 Corinthians 6:11; Romans 10:11.
[4] Isaiah 55:12; Romans 14:17; Romans 15:13.

May 30

My child:
I'm guiding your walk.[1]
Each day I prepare a table before you.[2]
If you choose what I have set before you,
you will be satisfied.
Do not attempt
to eat what is on someone else's table
or what is on your table for tomorrow.

---

[1] Psalm 32:8 (NLT); Psalm 119:133; John 16:13.
[2] Psalm 23:5.

May 31

My treasure, my love:
Today is a good day to bask in my love.[1]
There really is nothing more important than this!
It is the beginning place, my love.
Everything else emanates from there.
Make basking in my love a priority.
Make it a way of life.
It is your medicine.
It is your life source.
Drink of my love and be well.

---

[1] 1 John 4:16; John 15:9-17; Romans 5:5.

June

June 1

Dear friend:

It is difficult for you to see my plan for your life.[1]

I invite you to take a look with me

from our vantage point in the heavenly places.[2]

You see yourself as an insignificant person with no power.

But look, I have gifted you with my Spirit –

you have my power and authority resident within you.[3]

When you speak, you speak my words.

Do not doubt this.

Furthermore, it is not an accident

that you are where you are.

I have placed you there to accomplish my purposes.

Do not withdraw in fear and uncertainty.

Accept with confidence the place I have given you.[4]

---

[1] Jeremiah 29:11; Psalm 138:8 (NLT).
[2] Ephesians 2:6; Colossians 3:1.
[3] John 14:26; 2 Timothy 1:14; 1 Corinthians 3:16; Ephesians 3:20; Titus 3:6.
[4] Ephesians 4:1; Ephesians 2:10.

June 2

My treasure, my love:
You are experiencing a period of transition.
It is a transition
from independence to surrender.[1]
It is a transition
from relying on yourself to relying on me.[2]
It is a transition
from thinking that you are in charge and have control
to realizing that I am Lord[3]
and having personal control is mostly an illusion.[4]
You are in that uncomfortable place
where the old way of self-reliance is not working anymore
and you are still learning how to rely on me.

---

[1] Luke 22:42; Matthew 6:10.
[2] Proverbs 3:5;
[3] Romans 14:11; Philippians 2:9-11.
[4] Proverbs 16:9.

June 3

My treasure, my sweetheart:
I am right here with you in this pain.[1]
Let's endure it together.
I was with you when you were experiencing harm.
My love did not protect you from being wounded,
but it sustained you.
My love has sustained you through all these years
and it will sustain you
as you continue on this healing journey.
Let's endure it together.
"They that sow in tears (will) reap in joy"[2] – you'll see.
So take a big breath, lift up your head, and be glad.
Be very glad because you will reap in joy,
my love, my sweetheart, my dove.

---

[1] Isaiah 41:10; Isaiah 43:2; Matthew 28:20b.
[2] Psalm 126:5 (English Revised Version – ERV).

June 4

My treasure, my love:
Lift up your heart and be glad!
I have every intention
of answering every one of your prayers.[1]
Now is not the time to give up![2]
I am at work.
Sometimes things have to get worse
before they can get better.
In the end you will see this, so why not rejoice now?
Why not trust that I know what I am doing
and that it will all work out for good in the end?[3]
When you have done that,
then you will be able to resume your work
on the task I have given you.
Do not focus on all these works in process –
you will not see in them what you desire.
Instead, focus on my power and might and love,
through which I will accomplish
more than you can ask or imagine![4]
Yes, I will do more than you can ask or imagine!
You'll see.
For now, surrender all your loved ones and your cares
into my loving hands and rejoice.[5]
Rejoice and relax.

---

[1] Matthew 7:7-8.
[2] Luke 18:1-8; Galatians 6:9.
[3] Romans 8:28.
[4] Ephesians 3:20.
[5] Philippians 4:4; 1 Thessalonians 5:16.

June 5

Treasure:
I am giving you compassion.
As you dwell in my heart,[1]
you are surrounded by compassion –
immersed in it.[2]
The greatest obstacle
to your experiencing compassion
is self-centeredness.
So lose yourself in me,[3]
find your complete identity in me,
and realize that apart from me, you are nothing.

---

[1] Romans 13:14; Galatians 3:27.
[2] 1 John 4:16.
[3] John 15:1-17.

June 6

My treasure, my love:
Still and quiet your soul,[1] my love.
All is well.
You are safe in my love.[2]
You can make a multitude of mistakes
and nothing of value changes!
This is grace[3] – unmerited favor.
I extend it to you.
Extend it to yourself, my love.
And move on!
Don't let this soul work[4]
keep you from proceeding
with my plan for your life.
Enjoy everything I am giving you these days.
Continue to do your work with excellence
and I will lead you to the next challenge.
Follow your heart and you will be right on track![5]

---

[1] Psalm 131:2; Psalm 62:5; Psalm 130:5.
[2] Psalm 91; Romans 8:38-39; Jude 1:21 (NLT).
[3] Hebrews 4:15-16.
[4] Philippians 2:12.
[5] Ezekiel 36:26-27; Galatians 5:16; Colossians 2:6-7.

June 7

My treasure, my love:
This is a time when I am carrying you.[1]
I am holding you close in my arms.[2]
I am whispering endearments in your ear.[3]
Let me nurture you with my love.
Let me heal you with my love.[4]

---

[1] Isaiah 46:4; Deuteronomy 1:30-31.
[2] Psalm 17:8.
[3] Zephaniah 3:17 (NLT).
[4] Isaiah 53:5.

June 8

My treasure, my love:
You are all in a dither –
let me soothe you with my love.[1]
You are doing the Martha thing,[2]
and it really is not necessary.
Let me gently remind you
that I've got everything in order.[3]
I really do have every detail in place.
You'll see.
Every detail in every area of your life is in place.
I've left nothing to chance.
You know how painstakingly I planned for my Son's life.[4]
I've taken the same care in planning your life.[5]
Choose to surrender to my will in everything.[6]

---

[1] Zephaniah 3:17 (NLT).
[2] Luke 10:38-42.
[3] Hebrews 1:3a; Colossians 1:16-17.
[4] This is a reference to the many prophecies that were fulfilled regarding the birth and life of Christ.
[5] Psalm 138:8 (NLT).
[6] Luke 22:42; Matthew 6:10.

June 9

Dear friend:
I am blessing future generations through you in many ways.
As you simply obey me each day, this is happening.
Continue to serve and love me,
and you will be used by me to bless future generations.
Follow the desires I have placed in your heart
and love others into life.
Begin right now with the people in your current acquaintance.
Love is the key that unlocks the door to past hurts,
the medicine that heals.
Only love will cure.
Only love will provide lasting healing.
Lavishly pour out my love on all around you.[1]
Extravagantly waste it on all –
and you will be astounded by what happens.
This is my way – to love my creation into life
and you are one through whom I choose to do this.
Give yourself completely to me for this purpose,
and you will leave a legacy of incalculable wealth
for future generations.

---

[1] 1 Thessalonians 3:12; Philippians 1:9; John 15:12; 1 Corinthians 13.

June 10

Treasure, regarding decision-making:
Trust your desires, for I am in you,
causing you to know my pleasure.[1]
Relax about this.
Consult me when I ask you to,
but otherwise assume we are working together.[2]
You have not yet grasped the fact that my life is your life[3] –
you have no other.
I will convict you when you are being motivated
by the enemy[4] or your old sin nature.[5]
Rest in me.[6]
I am working in you in all my glorious strength[7]
so relax and enjoy it!

---

[1] Philippians 2:13.
[2] Matthew 11:29-30.
[3] Galatians 2:20.
[4] John 16:8.
[5] Romans 6:1-14.
[6] Matthew 11:28-29.
[7] Ephesians 18-20; Romans 6:4; 2 Peter 1:3.

June 11

Dear one:
I have created the sexual union of a married couple
to express the intimacy of the relationship
I desire to have with my children.
It is holy; it is sacred.
It is a time to celebrate my presence in a special way.
It is a time to rejoice in my creativity
and in my desire to commune with my children.
I repeat – this is a most holy and sacred act
and a time when I am most assuredly present,
rejoicing and delighting in my creation.
I rejoice in this full and complete expression
of physical, emotional and spiritual oneness.
It is to be enjoyed,
for I have created it for pleasure
and for spiritual renewal.
I am most intimately a part of this sacred union
and use it to bless and to renew.[1]

---

[1] See the Song of Solomon for God's view of sex.

June 12

Today I will speak to you regarding control. I am your God.[1] Your life is in my hands[2] – have you not continually placed it there? Trust me to order your days.[3]

Your life is not a haphazard collection of isolated events as you suppose. I am a master crafter: I plan each detail in advance, and when the time is right, I execute every event. I have planned a masterpiece for your life – known only to me. It will be revealed in its exquisite beauty as time unfolds. Imagine an intricate carving: Each detail is painstakingly worked until the design, known in advance only to the crafter, gradually appears.

Dear one – I am the master crafter of your life. Trust me to create a work of infinite beauty. Keep your eyes on your Creator, and in the end, you will behold the masterpiece I have woven with each thread of your life. Trust me, my dear one! With infinite care and patience I plan and execute every detail. With great skill I work even your mistakes into my design, for I am great and mighty to accomplish all that I set out to do.[4]

Dear child – I have before my eyes my plan for your life.[5] I view it with great excitement in my heart. I will share it with you when you join me in heaven and you will worship me with awe and joy at the splendor of the masterpiece I have created.

Bless me, my child, for I have accomplished this for my glory and our great joy.

Little one – relinquish control, surrender your life to my creativity, and live!

---

[1] Ezekiel 34:31; Psalm 100:3.
[2] Isaiah 49:2; Isaiah 51:16; Isaiah 62:3.
[3] Psalm 138:8 (NLT).
[4] Philippians 1:6.
[5] Jeremiah 29:11.

June 13

Treasure:
Let my Kingdom be your primary concern.[1]
I will handle all the details of your life.[2]
I do not want my children to get bogged down
with the mundane necessities of life,
for to touch these is to touch death.
Walk above these things
in the exciting activities of the Kingdom.
You know by now the joy you experience when you do this –
I want you to always live in this joy.
I am El Shaddai[3] –
strong and mighty to act on your behalf—
so do not bore yourself
with what you shall eat, drink, wear or where you should live.
Be casual about this, confident that I will provide.[4]

---

[1] Matthew 6:33; John 6:27-29.
[2] Psalm 138:8 (NLT).
[3] Genesis 17:1 (NLT); Exodus 6:3 (NLT).
[4] Philippians 4:19; 1 Timothy 6:17.

June 14

My treasure, my love:
I am with you in this painful place.[1]
It is good to acknowledge wrongdoing
and to cry tears of remorse.[2]
I see your tears and I receive them.
Surrender your tears and your grief to me.
I have already taken them on my cross.[3]
I also have taken your guilt and sin on my cross,
so hand them to me also.[4]
I did this so you could be free
from the burden of sin and guilt, grief and shame.[5]
There is no good purpose served in continuing to grieve.
There definitely is no good purpose
in hating yourself for what you have done!
You have learned to hate the sin others perpetrate
while respecting and appreciating the sinner.
Extend this same grace towards yourself.
My treasure, I am creating beauty
out of even this experience in your life.[6]
So surrender this pain to me.
Breathe deeply.
Put on your multi-colored coat of iridescent joy,[7]
and move into this day with hope in your heart!
I love you, my treasure, my joy, my delight![8]

---

[1] Matthew 28:20b.
[2] Psalm 32:5; Proverbs 28:13;
[3] Isaiah 53:4.
[4] Isaiah 53:5.
[5] 1 John 1:9.
[6] Isaiah 61:3; Romans 8:28.
[7] Genesis 37:3 (English Standard Version – ESV); Psalm 30:11 (NLT).
[8] 1 John 4:16; Zephaniah 3:17 (NLT); Psalm 147:11 (NLT).

June 15

My treasure, my love:
Let me show you things from my perspective.
From my perspective, all is well.
I have everything in hand.[1]
None of the things you fear are in my plan.
My plans are for good and not for disaster.[2]
Give me all these things you hate
and I will create beauty out of the ashes.[3]
I will create beauty out of the ashes
of each of these experiences you find so unacceptable.
Everything you hate and everything you fear –
give it to me.
Entrust it all into my care
and watch for beauty to emerge.

---

[1] Hebrews 1:3a; Colossians 1:16-17.
[2] Jeremiah 29:11.
[3] Isaiah 61:3.

June 16

My love:
Let me be clear about your reality.
You are not overcome by grief.
What is happening in your soul—
in your mind, your will, and your emotions—
is not what is happening in your new life.[1]
In your real life,
your new life in Christ,[2]
you are overcome by joy.
My joy, in fact, is your strength in this situation.[3]
Do not let what is happening in your soul
dictate your experience.

---

[1] Romans 6:4; Titus 3:5 (NLT); Colossians 3:1; 2 Corinthians 5:17; 1 Peter 1:3.
[2] Colossians 3:1-3.
[3] Nehemiah 8:10.

June 17

My treasure, my love:
Have you taken your stand?[1]
Know that I have prepared a place for you to stand.
Know this, my love!
It is a place for you and for no other.
It is a place for now.
I have prepared this place for you
and I have prepared you for this place.[2]
Don't be afraid to take your place.[3]
Let all your thoughts be hope-filled.
Let all your thoughts be joy-filled.
Let all your thoughts
be imbued with gratitude
and motivated by love
as you take your stand.

---

[1] Romans 11:29; Ephesians 2:10.
[2] Hebrews 13:21; Philippians 2:13.
[3] 2 Timothy 1:6-7.

June 18

My love, my treasure:
I have kept you through this challenge.[1]
It's been my pleasure to keep you through it all!
And now we are going to put it all together
and make sense of it all!
Yes, we are!!
We are going to bring great good out of it all.[2]
You and I will work together on this.
You can count on me to keep you through this
just as I have kept you through your entire life.
Throw back your head and laugh, my love.
I plan to bring together all the strands of your life
into a beautiful tapestry.[3]
You will be amazed and delighted.
So keep on believing in me[4] and trusting me.[5]
And I'll keep on keeping you, my treasure.

---

[1] 1 Corinthians 1:8; Jude 1:24.
[2] Romans 8:28.
[3] Psalm 138:8 (NLT).
[4] John 6:29.
[5] Proverbs 3:5.

June 19

My treasure:
I am delighted to receive your requests.
Leave these things with me and relax.[1]
Today I want to talk with you
about what you say about others.
You know that I have instructed you
to fix your thoughts on what is positive.[2]
Let these same characteristics
guide what you say about others.
In this way
you will avoid colluding with the enemy
whose intent is to steal, kill, and destroy human life.[3]

---

[1] Philippians 4:6.
[2] Philippians 4:8.
[3] John 10:10.

June 20

My treasure, my love:
Give me your full attention.
Yes, look to me with complete and single-minded focus.[1]
What you will find is unconditional delight –
I am unconditionally delighted in you![2]
You have absolutely nothing to fear.
I am fully engaged in every detail of your life.[3]
I am providing and protecting you
with attention to the minutiae.
So lift up your head and be glad.
Throw off everything that drags you down.[4]
Free yourself from all bondage and burdens.
And rejoice in my love.
Rejoice in my delight in you.

---

[1] Psalm 141:8; Hebrews 12:2; Hebrews 3:1.
[2] Psalm 37:23; Psalm 147:11; Psalm 149:4; Zephaniah 3:17 (NLT).
[3] Psalm 138:8 (NLT); Philippians 1:6.
[4] Hebrews 12:1.

June 21

My treasure, my love:
Keep your eyes on your goal.[1]
See it very clearly.
Don't let current circumstances deter you.
Keep believing
that you already have received
what you desire.[2]
Keep trusting that we are in this together.[3]
And keep doing what you know to do.
One more thing:
Be motivated by love —[4]
Love always hopes, always believes, and always endures.[5]
Do this out of love for the people
who will be blessed through your efforts.
I know these people by name.
I know how they will be blessed.
I'm excited about this and you can be too!

---

[1] Philippians 3:13-14; 1 Corinthians 9:26 (NLT).
[2] Mark 11:24.
[3] Matthew 11:29.
[4] 1 Corinthians 16:14; Ephesians 5:2.
[5] 1 Corinthians 13:7.

June 22

You are believing the lie
that you can't be okay if someone disapproves of you.
You are believing the lie
that you need to have approval.
You are believing the lie
that your well-being depends on receiving favor.
These lies are just that – lies![1]
You do not need approval from anyone
to be peaceful, joyful, and content.
In your spirit right now
you **are** peaceful, joyful, and content.
It is in your soul
that you believe these lies
and experience torment.
Tune in to your spirit
where you commune with my Spirit
and enjoy serenity.[2]
This is what it means
to "(be) still, and know that I am God."[3]

---

[1] Proverbs 29:25; Isaiah 51:12.
[2] John 14:23; 1 Corinthians 3:16.
[3] Psalm 46:10a (ESV).

June 23

My love, my treasure:
Keep it really simple.
Don't try to figure it out.[1]
Be like a child
who expects an all-knowing, wise, loving,
and extravagantly generous parent
to provide everything at all times.[2]
Expect me to motivate and cause you
to do what I want you to do.[3]
Just don't worry about anything![4]

---

[1] Psalm 131:1; Psalm 139:6.
[2] Philippians 4:19.
[3] Philippians 2:13.
[4] Luke 12:22; Philippians 4:6.

June 24

My treasure:

You are deeply loved.[1]

Negative circumstances

do not make the slightest dint

in my love for you.

You can revel and bask in my love for you at all times!

Come close to me,

let my strong arms enfold you,

lean your head on my chest,

and relax.[2]

Breathe deeply, my love, as you surrender

to what I provide in your life through circumstances.[3]

All is well.

It's all good.

I make all things good.[4]

Let go

and enjoy this beautiful day

I have made for you.[5]

---

[1] 1 John 4:16; John 15:9-17; Romans 5:5.

[2] Psalm 91:4.

[3] Luke 22:42; Matthew 6:10.

[4] Romans 8:28.

[5] Psalm 118:24.

June 25

My lovely one:
Thank you for pouring out your heart to me.
Wholeness begins
with courageous and honest acknowledgment
of your personal experience –
there is no point in denying what you are truly feeling.
The end of the story of your life has not yet been written.
Well, it **has** been written in my Book of Life,[1]
but you have not yet lived it!
Today I am giving you the opportunity
to experience the joy
that ensues from godliness with contentment.[2]
Choose to be content with your life exactly as it is today.[3]

[1] Psalm 139:16; Philippians 4:3; Revelation 3:5; Revelation 20:12.
[2] 1 Timothy 6:6
[3] Philippians 4:11.

June 26

My love, my treasure:

In your spirit, you are serene.

There can be ferocious storms on the surface of the ocean

while serene stillness reigns down below.

Learn to let go of all that is not stillness.

This is what it means to "(be) still, and know that I am God."[1]

My treasure: All the days of your life are written in my book.[2]

I have many blessings in store for you.[3]

I will redeem everything the locust has eaten.[4]

No sacrifice you have made will go unnoticed.

I even record all your tears![5]

Lift up your head and rejoice, my love.

I am bringing you to a very pleasant place.[6]

Learn to believe

that you have received what you have requested

and it will be yours![7]

---

[1] Psalm 46:10a (ESV).
[2] Psalm 139:16.
[3] Deuteronomy 28:8; Philippians 4:19.
[4] Joel 2:25.
[5] Psalm 56:8.
[6] Psalm 23:2; Psalm 36:5-9.
[7] Mark 11:24.

June 27

So many distressful things
caught your attention today, my love.
When this happens,
check in with Jesus to see how he wants to pray.[1]
Then, with joy, lift up those requests to me
and leave the concern with me.[2]
These things are not for you to carry.
No.
Your life is to be characterized by freedom and joy.
Join me in my joy –
the joy that I have because I know
how everything will turn out in the end.[3]
I know the fabulous new earth I have planned
where there is no sorrow or pain.[4]

---

[1] Romans 8:34.
[2] Philippians 4:6-7.
[3] Psalm 16:11; John 15:11; Hebrews 12:2.
[4] Revelation 21:1-4.

June 28

My lovely one:
Do not fear.[1]
I have placed in your heart
my Spirit of love and power and a sound mind.[2]
Rejoice in this.
Celebrate this.
Confess this.
Claim this.
Do not settle for anything less.
Dear child, I am within you
in the same strength
that raised Jesus from the dead.[3]
Know that it is my will to set you totally free from fear.

---

[1] Isaiah 41:10, 13; Psalm 27:1; Romans 8:31.
[2] 2 Timothy 1:7; Titus 3:6.
[3] Romans 8:11, 15.

June 29

My treasure, my love:
Celebrate our oneness, my love.[1]
March boldly into this day together with me.
Your life is the life of Christ[2] who knows me completely:[3]
He knows my impeccable faithfulness.[4]
He knows the delight I take in blessing my children.[5]
He knows my meticulous attention to detail.[6]
He knows the fabulous plan I have for your life.[7]
Those who know they are my children[8]
can be free of worry.[9]
That's you!

---

[1] 1 John 4:15; John 14:23; John 17:20-23; Revelation 3:20.
[2] Galatians 2:20; Ephesians 3:16-17.
[3] Matthew 11:27; John 7:28-29.
[4] Lamentations 3:22-23; Psalm 89:2; Psalm 119:90.
[5] Deuteronomy 28:1-14; Psalm 149:4.
[6] Psalm 37:23 (NLT); 2 Samuel 23:5 (NLT).
[7] Jeremiah 29:11; Psalm 138:8 (NLT).
[8] John 1:12; Galatians 3:26; Ephesians 1:5.
[9] Isaiah 26:3, 12; Philippians 4:7.

June 30

My treasure, my love:
Today was a challenging day
where things did not turn out as you anticipated.
It provided you with an opportunity
to surrender what was happening to me.[1]
It's good to surrender to me everything that happens –
whether it appears good or bad or of no import.
Even now – surrender it all to me.
Your job was to respond as best you could,
and this is exactly what you did.
So, it's all good.
Let it all go into the archives of history.
It was as it was, and it is finished.

---

[1] Psalm 37:5; Proverbs 3:5.

July

July 1

My treasure:

Do not despair.

I am working patience and long-suffering in you.[1]

Know this:

I am your God

and I will show myself strong on your behalf.[2]

Lay aside your stress and striving

and watch to see what I will do.

Detach yourself from this situation –

do not let yourself be moved by circumstances.

Am I not God?

Is my arm too short to save?[3]

Rejoice in me.

I will lead you through this Red Sea.[4]

This situation is temporary.

This storm will pass.

I will move in supernaturally

and do a marvelous thing

to reveal my glory.[5]

---

[1] Colossians 1:9-12; James 1:2-3.
[2] 2 Chronicles 16:9a.
[3] Numbers 11:23; Isaiah 59:1.
[4] Exodus 13-14.
[5] John 9:3; John 11:40.

July 2

My child, celebrate my love for you.[1] Bask in it. Know that it is never-ending and all-powerful.[2]

Know this, child of mine: My love for you is not contingent on what you do in my Kingdom. I love you because I **am** love – it is my being.[3] My love is extended to all of my creation. Those who choose to believe in my Son know my love because I dwell in them and they in me.[4] The work you do is merely an expression of that love we share.[5] Remain in my love by letting this love pour out to others as you are doing.

Do not look to the right or to the left – know that I have honored your request to be your guide, and I have placed you squarely on the path I have chosen for you.[6] Enjoy it. Pursue excellence in it. Know this also – I am going before you and preparing a way.[7] I am creating favor for you. Take advantage of every opportunity to learn and grow and bless. Do not spend even one second looking at what others do, for I have not gifted you and graced you to walk in their paths, but only in yours.[8]

My lovely one: Worship me, praise me, bless me, for in this you will find your reason for being.[9] Celebrate your intimacy with me. "Delight yourself in (me, and I) will give you the desires of your heart."[10]

---

[1] 1 John 4:16; John 15:9-17; Romans 5:5.
[2] 1 Corinthians 13:8.
[3] 1 John 4:16.
[4] John 14:23.
[5] John 15:1-17.
[6] Psalm 32:8 (NLT); Proverbs 3:6. Deuteronomy 31:8; Psalm 139:16.
[7] Deuteronomy 31:8
[8] John 21:20-22.
[9] 1 Peter 2:9.
[10] Psalm 37:4 (ESV).

July 3

Dear friend:
You are asking how I managed to embrace the cross.
That is such a good question!
I sweated blood as I agonized over enduring the cross![1]
Eventually I surrendered to my Father's will,[2]
but it wasn't easy.
Part of me was saying, "Please, let it not be this way!"
But another part of me was saying, "It has to be this way."
It's the same with you.
In your soul you are saying,
"It can't be this way. I can't handle this."
In your spirit you know it has to be this way.
This is the way that God has ordained.[3]
So, I get this struggle you're having, my love.
Eventually you will surrender to what God has ordained
and then you will experience peace.[4]

[1] Luke 22:44.
[2] Luke 22:42.
[3] Ephesians 2:10.
[4] John 14:26-27; John 16:33.

July 4

My treasure, my love:
Put yourself in agreement with me
and love yourself.[1]
Love yourself unconditionally.
You and I know that you are doing your best,
And that is enough!
That is **enough** I say!
Love yourself,
treasure yourself,
enjoy yourself.
Learn to laugh at yourself –
find amusing and endearing
all your little idiosyncrasies.
I do![2]

---

[1] Mark 12:31.
[2] Zephaniah 3:17 (NLT).

July 5

My treasure, my love:
Continue to fill your mind and heart
with positive thoughts and images
that reflect your intentions.
Faith can move mountains and you will experience this.[1]
Let me give you a great example of this:
Counting the joy that lay before him,
Jesus endured the cross.[2]
How do you think he "counted the joy?"
Practically speaking, what did he do?
Yes.
He filled his mind and heart
with images of what he expected to experience
as a result of his sacrifice.
He was filled with joy
as he imagined the redemption of countless people.
That's how he did it and that's how you can do it.
That's how you believe
that you have received what you have requested.
It's fun, my love! Enjoy this process.

[1] Matthew 17:20.
[2] Hebrews 12:2.

July 6

Be still in my presence for a while, my love.[1]
Let my presence within you still your soul.[2]
Let my presence within you
bring healing to your body.[3]
Let my presence within you
bring a refreshing, a rejuvenating,
and a rekindling of your passion.[4]
Drink, my love.
Drink deeply of my life, of my love, of my joy!
Let your self be renewed in me.[5]
I am the great I AM.[6]
There is none other than I.[7]

---

[1] Psalm 37:7a; Psalm 62:5.
[2] Zephaniah 3:17 (NLT).
[3] Romans 8:11.
[4] Psalm 19:7; Psalm 23:3.
[5] Colossians 3:10.
[6] Exodus 3:14.
[7] Deuteronomy 4:35; Isaiah 44:6; 1 Corinthians 8:6.

July 7

Child of mine:
You are the apple of my eye,[1]
and I am leading and guiding you continuously.[2]
I am transforming you into my image.[3]
I am purifying your heart.[4]
You have developed a debilitating habit
of negative self-talk and self-doubt.
Your self-doubt is making it difficult for you to do
what I have designed for you to do.
You are looking to others for affirmation
that must come from within.
It is time to change this
by daily affirming
the positive qualities and characteristics
I created in you.
I expect you to love yourself first,
and then to love others as you love yourself.[5]
If you are critical of yourself,
you will be critical of others.
If you are positive and affirming towards yourself,
you will be this way towards others.
So learn to affirm yourself, to build yourself up, to love yourself,
and then you will be set free to love others.

---

[1] Psalm 17:8; Zechariah 2:8; Deuteronomy 32:10.
[2] Isaiah 58:11.
[3] 2 Corinthians 3:18.
[4] Psalm 66:10.
[5] Matthew 22:39.

July 8

Treasure:
I am at work in the lives of all my children –
repentant and rebellious.[1]
My love is not conditional.[2]
I am merciful and compassionate,
gracious and gentle.[3]
I do not break a bruised reed or smother a smoldering wick.[4]
My way is to encourage, to enable, to heal, and to deliver.
Do not be discouraged or upset
about what is happening in your life –
simply continue to reach out to me in faith.
I am providing for you all that you need.[5]

---

[1] Psalm 139; Jeremiah 23:23-24; Acts 17:27.
[2] Matthew 5:45; Psalm 145:9.
[3] Exodus 34:6; Matthew 11:29; Matthew 21:5.
[4] Isaiah 42:3; Matthew 12:20.
[5] Psalm 23:1; 2 Corinthians 9:8; Matthew 6:33.

July 9

———————————————

What's in your heart is what's in mine,
for I dwell[1] in your heart.
Look within.
What are the yearnings, the longings, the deep desires?
Those are also mine.
Take courage, my child, to look.
Are you not created in my image?[2]
Is your life not the life of my Son?[3]
This is not a time for false modesty.
It is a time for bold presumption!
Be who you are!
Discover what's hidden in your heart,
and believe me to bring these desires into being.[4]

———————————————

[1] John 14:23; 2 Corinthians 4:7; 1 John 4:16; Revelation 3:20.
[2] Genesis 1:27.
[3] Galatians 2:20.
[4] Psalm 21:2; Psalm 37:4; Matthew 21:22.

July 10

My love, I am pleased when you take time to still your soul and listen to me speak in your spirit.[1]

Today I wish to speak to you about ministry. Ministry flows from my heart that dwells within you. It is always motivated by love.[2] It is never self-seeking and always produces the fruit of righteousness, peace, and joy.[3] Judge all ministry by these standards:

- Is it motivated by love?
- Does it produce righteousness, peace, and joy?

I am so pleased to dwell within you! Celebrate my presence continually. Look to me to be your resource in all circumstances.[4]

---

[1] Psalm 131:2; Psalm 62:5; Psalm 130:5; Proverbs 1:23; John 16:13.
[2] Romans 5:5; 1 Corinthians 16:14.
[3] Romans 14:17, Galatians 5:22.
[4] 2 Corinthians 9:8.

July 11

Precious friend:
You are feeling desperate.
That is not from me;
I am experiencing joy and contentment.
You are experiencing concern.
That is not from me;
I am experiencing confidence and certainty.
I am certain of the blessings I have planned for you.[1]
I am confident in the future I see for you.[2]
Remember that your real life is hidden with me in God.[3]
Turn from the desperation and concern
you are experiencing in your soul,
fix your eyes on me,[4]
and live your real life:
joyful, content, confident, and certain.

---

[1] Psalm 21:6; 1 Timothy 6:17.
[2] Jeremiah 29:11.
[3] Colossians 3:3.
[4] Hebrews 12:2.

July 12

My treasure, my love:
You have been reborn by my Spirit,[1]
so when you look inside,
you find me in intimate communion with you.[2]
You have not become divine,
but you have been set free
to commune with me and to reflect my nature.[3]
Wherever you go,
I will provide faithful friends to support you
just as I am providing the support you need now.
My plan for you is to give you a future and a hope.[4]
Keep looking to me, putting your hope in me.[5]

---

[1] John 1:12-13; John 3:1-21; 1 Peter 1:23.
[2] John 14:23; John 17:20-23; 1 John 4:15; Revelation 3:20.
[3] 2 Corinthians 3:18; Romans 8:29.
[4] Jeremiah 29:11.
[5] Psalm 39:7 (NIV).

July 13

My love, my treasure—I am within you,[1]
enjoying you, inspiring you, loving you.
Relax in my love.
If only you could perceive the extent of my love for you!
Then you would never be afraid.
You would never doubt.
You would never be upset!
Keep seeking me and greater revelation of my love for you.[2]
I am not upset with your expression of frustrations.
Feelings indicate situations that need attention.
Try to be motivated by my love in all you do.[3]
Know that I am leading and guiding you your struggles.[4]
I work in all circumstances to bring good.[5]
I agree with the approach you are taking
regarding listening to me.
It is a humble and sensible approach:
listen, check what you hear
against scripture and your knowledge of me,
wait for circumstances to line up,
and move beyond mistakes to trying again.
Just as Jesus learned obedience,
so you are learning to hear my voice.[6]
Enjoy the process!
I have such excitement in my relationship with you!
Join me in my excitement.
Let's have fun together, daily defeating the enemy
with his poverty, negativity, despair, doubt,
disease, confusion, impatience, etc.

---

[1] John 14:23; 2 Corinthians 4:7; 1 John 4:15; Revelation 3:20.
[2] Ephesians 3:16-19; Romans 8:38-39.
[3] Romans 5:5; 1 Corinthians 16:14.
[4] Psalm 73:23-24; Isaiah 58:11.
[5] Romans 8:28.
[6] Hebrews 5:8.

July 14

My child:
It delights me that you draw near to me[1] –
that you want to hear from me,
that you want to be one with me.
I am your light,[2] your life,[3] your bread.[4]
I want you to learn to love yourself [5]–
to walk in forgiveness towards yourself.[6]
I also want you to walk in forgiveness towards your family.
Resentment and judgment are cousins.
Choose to uncover any resentments,
beginning first with yourself,
then with your family,
and then with others.
This is unfinished business from the past
that is keeping you trapped in old ways of being.
Try dealing with resentments, my love,
and you will discover a key to being set free.

---

[1] James 4:8a; Hebrews 10:22.
[2] John 8:12.
[3] John 11:25; John 14:6.
[4] John 6:35, 48.
[5] Mark 12:31.
[6] Matthew 6:12.

July 15

My treasure, bring me your questions.
I will shine a light on your path.[1]
I am using this area of finances
to transform you into the image of my Son.[2]
This comes with pressure, with the refining work of fire.[3]
Each time, the fire is hotter and the pressure is greater.
I am looking for a people who will not waver in their trust
no matter how great the pressure.
I am creating a people who will not doubt my love
no matter how desperate their circumstances.[4]
So stand firm.
Do not doubt.
Believe my Word.
You know me - you have proven me over and over.
Stand firm in this.

[1] Psalm 18:28; Psalm 119:105.
[2] 2 Corinthians 3:18.
[3] Malachi 3:2-3; Psalm 66:10.
[4] James 1:2-8.

July 16

My love, my treasure:
Yes, yes, yes!!
I truly have kept you through the dark night of the soul![1]
And I can't think of anywhere I'd rather have been
than right there with you!
My love, my treasure –
we have been through a lot, you and I.
We have been through a lot.
Nothing can separate us.[2]
You know that.
You know that wherever you go,
I am there.[3]

---

[1] Psalm 23:4; Luke 1:78-79.
[2] Romans 8:38-39.
[3] Psalm 139:7-12; Matthew 28:20b.

July 17

Dear friend:

You are meditating on Paul's encouragement to pray continuously[1] and thinking that if that is what you are to do, then I also must have prayed continuously when I lived on earth. Praying continuously seems like an impossible task to you, and you are asking me how I managed to do it.

Prayer is being in communion with God, being connected with God. Because my being was in God,[2] was emanating from God,[3] everything I did or thought or felt was prayer.

It's the same with you, my beautiful friend. You are in me; I am in you.[4] Your life is my life; my life is your life. You may not be aware of it, but you **are** praying continuously.

You can do things to help you be more aware of our communion or to enrich our communion, but that oneness is a given.

And I love it! It was counting **this** joy that I endured the cross.[5]

You know full well when you do something that disrupts our oneness. Simple confession immediately repairs the breech[6] and you are back to your default mode of praying continuously.

---

[1] 1 Thessalonians 5:17.
[2] John 14:11; John 17:21.
[3] John 1:14; John 8:42; John 16:28.
[4] Galatians 2:20; Romans 8:10; Colossians 3:3; 1 John 4:16.
[5] Hebrews 12:2.
[6] 1 John 1:9.

July 18

My child:

Seek my face to know my will,[1]

yield to the leading and guidance of my Spirit,[2]

and leave the results to me.[3]

Many times I use you to sow seeds.

The harvest will come later, and you may or may not see it.

Do your best and leave it.

You may analyze what you have done

in order to learn and grow,

but not to condemn yourself.[4]

You simply do not have adequate information to judge –

there are so many things happening that you cannot know.

Assume the best.

Trust me to protect you from all harm.[5]

---

[1] Romans 12:2; Colossians 1:9-12.

[2] Ezekiel 36:27; Romans 8:9.

[3] Isaiah 49:4.

[4] Romans 8:1.

[5] Psalm 32:7; Psalm 91:10; Psalm 121:7; 2 Timothy 4:18.

July 19

Treasure, you have received the news
that there is a suspicion of cancer in your body.
So here you are at my feet,
asking me to come to talk with you about this.
I would love to come and talk with you!
Not that I have far to come – I'm already here![1]
I haven't left you for one second.
And I won't leave you. Ever.[2]
Please don't be afraid.[3]
Instead, lose yourself in my love.[4]
See your self enveloped and imbued with my love.
See your self strengthened and energized
and healed by my love.
See this circumstance as an opportunity
to demonstrate faith
and to reveal my glory.[5]
Yes, the glory of God will be revealed through this circumstance.

---

[1] John 14:23; John 17:20-23; 1 John 4:15; Revelation 3:20.
[2] Matthew 28:20b.
[3] Matthew 14:27; Mark 5:36.
[4] John 15:1-17.
[5] John 9:2-3; John 11:4,40.

July 20

God is on the throne.[1]
Regardless of what happens –
God is on the throne.
Kingdoms come and kingdoms go,
but God is on the throne.
God is not moved by anything.[2]
God's Word never passes away.[3]
God is on the throne.

---

[1] Psalm 47:8; Hebrews 1:8.
[2] Isaiah 54:10; Isaiah 51:6.
[3] Mark 13:31.

July 21

My darling, my love:
I have never left you.[1]
I have never stopped speaking to you.
I communicate with you in and through all you do and are.
Sometimes you still and quiet your soul
in a deliberate effort to hear my voice[2] – this is good, too.
My child, even when you think I am not speaking to you,
the silence carries my voice –
there is something being communicated in the silence.
You love to quote Philippians 2:13.
This truly is what is happening in your life,
and even when you are not aware of it.
So relax!
Draw close to me,[3] enjoy our oneness,[4] and stop fretting!
Don't worry about your current project –
I am motivating you to do what you need to do.[5]
Just enjoy it.
Let yourself be filled and surrounded by my love,[6]
for it is through my love
that you live and move and have your being.[7]
One last thing, my treasure:
Do not worry about money.[8]
I am your Shepherd and will provide all that you need.[9]
"Be still, and know that I am God."[10]

---

[1] Matthew 28:20b.
[2] Psalm 131:2; Psalm 62:5; Psalm 130:5.
[3] Psalm 73:28; Matthew 11:28-29; Hebrews 10:22; James 4:8a.
[4] John 14:23; John 17:20-23; 1 John 4:16; Revelation 3:20.
[5] Philippians 2:13.
[6] 1 John 4:16.
[7] Acts 17:28.
[8] Matthew 6:25; Philippians 4:6.
[9] Psalm 23:1; John 10:11.
[10] Psalm 46:10a (ESV).

July 22

My lovely one, my child:
To rest is your inheritance.[1]
You can rest in the finished work of Jesus on the cross.[2]
To rest means to cease all striving,
to be at peace,
to know your position in Christ,
to know no fear, only love.
So enter my rest.
Know that any battle you find yourself in is my battle.[3]
What I require of you is to draw close to me,[4]
and to trust that I am working in and through all things
to effect my good purpose.[5]
At one and the same time,
I am working in your life
and in the lives of those I bring into your life.[6]
Keep this in mind and be at peace.

---

[1] Hebrews 4:9-10.
[2] John 17:4.
[3] 1 Samuel 17:47; Zechariah 4:6.
[4] Psalm 73:28; Matthew 11:28-29; Hebrews 10:22; James 4:8a.
[5] Romans 8:28.
[6] Philippians 2:13.

July 23

My treasure, my love:
I am your all in all.[1]
I am your source.[2]
I am your beginning and your end.[3]
You do not yet fully see this,
but we are intimately connected,
you and I.
I in you and you in me[4] –
that's a riddle, isn't it?
And yet, it's a profound truth.
I in you and you in me.
There is no fear in that place, in that reality,
because it is the place of perfect love
and "perfect love casts out fear."[5]

---

[1] Colossians 1:16-17.
[2] Job 33:4; Psalm 16:2 (NLT).
[3] Revelation 22:13.
[4] 1 John 4:15.
[5] 1 John 4:18 (ESV).

July 24

My treasure, my love:
You wonder whether I have anything to say to you.
I always am communicating with you.
The question is, "Are you listening?!"
Today I would like to talk to you about missions,
about my children getting to know me as their loving parent.
If you want to know what is very dear to my heart, this is it.[1]
I have not created anyone
who I did not want to experience life as my child.[2]
I appreciate every little thing you do
to help my children draw closer to me.
The purpose behind every aspect of the work of the church
is to reconcile my children to me[3]
that they would experience and know me fully
in their bodies, minds, hearts, and souls.
Is there preaching? Dedicate it to this reconciling purpose.
Is there music? Dedicate it to this reconciling purpose.
Is there children's ministry?
Dedicate it to this reconciling purpose.
Is there healing ministry?
Dedicate it to this reconciling purpose.
Jesus came to reconcile my children to me.[4]
My heart's desire
is to enjoy an intimate relationship with each one.[5]
So: Be guided by this purpose.
Let it be a principle, a standard, a litmus test.
That joy that you experience when you are sharing scriptures with
those I send to you? That is my joy.
This is my heart that I am sharing with you today.

---

[1] 1 Timothy 2:3-4.
[2] Matthew 18:14.
[3] 2 Corinthians 5:17-20.
[4] Romans 5:10-11; 2 Corinthians 5:18.
[5] 2 Peter 3:9.

July 25

My treasure, my love:
"(Keep your eyes on) Jesus,
the author and the finisher of (your) faith."[1]
You are right to conclude that most of your fears arise from lies.
Replace those lies with my truth and you will be set free.[2]
"(My Son) came to destroy the works of the (evil one)."[3]
As he was obedient to me, he accomplished this.[4]
As you are obedient to me, you also accomplish this.
Do not worry about the devil.
Simply be obedient.
I will lead and guide you and you need simply to obey.[5]
Trust that I am giving you the information you need
as you need it.
My treasure – don't be troubled by this.
There is no trouble that can touch you except I allow it
and my plan for you is "to prosper you…
(and to) give you hope and a future."[6]
So relax. Rest in me.[7]
My treasure, my lovely:
Dwell only on the positives.[8]
Focus on all that is possible through me.[9]
Explore new options.
Be creative.
Be bold.

---

[1] Hebrews 12:2a (NHEB).
[2] John 8:31-32.
[3] 1 John 3:8b (NLT); John 8:44.
[4] Philippians 2:5-11.
[5] Psalm 32:8 (NLT); Psalm 48:14; Jeremiah 7:23; John 14:15.
[6] Jeremiah 29:11 (NIV).
[7] Matthew 11:28-29.
[8] Philippians 4:8.
[9] Matthew 19:26.

July 26

My treasure, my love:

Do not worry.[1] You have prayed and I have this situation in hand. So now, rest. "Be still, and know that I am God."[2]

Choose to believe. Choose to trust. You have done all that you can. I have given you faith;[3] exercise it.

You are thinking, "But this is a life and death matter." Yes. And so are all matters. That's what I deal with: Life and death issues. Life and death are in my hands. Trust me with this particular life and death issue.

You are second-guessing yourself. Stop. There is no good purpose in this. You asked me to fill you with my Spirit to equip you for this day and I did so.[4] You must choose to leave the outcome in my hands. You are thinking, "I have labored in vain. I have spent my strength for nothing at all."[5] And I say to you to leave with me the outcome and what is due you, your reward.

Let it go. You have been faithful. You have gone beyond the call of duty. Leave this in my hands.

Rest. Rest in me.[6] You can fall asleep in this boat.[7] The life of my Son within you[8] is already at rest. Join him. Relax. Have the same trust in me as he demonstrated when he walked the earth.

I have allowed this circumstance for your benefit as well.[9] Do what you know to do and then let it go.

---

[1] Philippians 4:6-7.
[2] Psalm 46:10a (ESV).
[3] Romans 12:3.
[4] Ephesians 5:18b; Titus 3:6.
[5] Isaiah 49:4a (NIV).
[6] Matthew 11:28-29.
[7] Mark 4:35-41.
[8] Galatians 2:20.
[9] Romans 8:28.

July 27

My treasure, my love:
Some things never change.
One of them is my love for you.
Even though you behaved in a very insulting way towards me,
I still love you.[1]
Even though you caused yourself
a great deal of misery with your behavior,
I still love you.
Yes, and I still am delighting in you with singing![2]
In fact, now my singing and rejoicing is amplified
by the saints in heaven
who always rejoice when a sinner repents.[3]
As for your confession, that was good.
That will be helpful to you and to others.[4]
And yes, I will heal you.
I will heal you of all the sickness this sin has caused.[5]
My treasure:
Draw near to me.[6]
Let me hold you in my heart.
Find rest for your soul.[7]

---

[1] Romans 5:8.
[2] Zephaniah 3:17.
[3] Luke 15:10.
[4] James 5:16.
[5] Psalm 103:3; Psalm 41:4.
[6] James 4:8a.
[7] Matthew 11:28-29.

July 28

My treasure, my love:
This is a very challenging time for you.
You are being called on to extend yourself
beyond what seems humanly possible.
I am carrying you, supporting you, and strengthening you.[1]
This time is temporary.
I am bringing you to a place of restoration and joy.[2]
Rest in me,[3] my love.
I will carry you through this travail to a much better place.

---

[1] Isaiah 46:4; Deuteronomy 1:30-31; Philippians 4:13.
[2] Psalm 23:3a; Isaiah 61:3; Psalm 51:12.
[3] Matthew 11:28-29.

July 29

My lovely one:
I love you,[1] and that's enough!

---

[1] 1 John 4:16.

July 30

My treasure:
If only you could know
the full extent of my love for you![1]
Then your fears would vanish.[2]
Vanish!
Meditate on my love for you.
Major on my love for you.
Recognize my love for you in everything.

---

[1] Psalm 36:5,7; Psalm 103:11 (NLT); Ephesians 3:17b-19.
[2] 1 John 4:18.

July 31

My treasure:

Look to me and live.[1]

Know that I have this situation in hand.[2]

I am accomplishing my purposes in and through it.[3]

Relax.

I am causing you to do what I desire of you.[4]

The only thing you need to change is your consternation!

Relax.

"Be still, and know that I am God."[5]

You do not have to have this situation in hand

because that is my job.

Know that I am God.

I am causing things to unfold as is best.

Know also that I will keep you safe.[6]

So relax.

Be happy and go to sleep.

---

[1] Isaiah 45:22.

[2] Hebrews 1:3a; Colossians 1:17.

[3] Psalm 33:11 (NLT); Isaiah 14:24; Isaiah 46:9-10; Ephesians 1:11.

[4] Philippians 2:13.

[5] Psalm 46:10a (ESV).

[6] Psalm 121:7-8; 2 Thessalonians 3:3; Jude 1:21 (NLT).

August

August 1

My treasure:
I am painstakingly shaping you,[1] my child,
to be free to love me with your entire being.
I am burning out the dross in your life[2] –
everything that keeps you from loving me.
Our love relationship is what matters most[3]
because this is eternal.
You need not concern yourself with this.
I am causing it to happen
and will continue in this work
until I have completed it.[4]
No amount of striving on your part
will add to this effort
or benefit it in any way.
Your job, your joy, is to trust and obey.
Let love,
our love,
my love for you and your love for me,
motivate you in all you do.[5]

---

[1] 2 Corinthians 3:18.
[2] Malachi 3:2-3; Psalm 66:10.
[3] Jude 1:21.
[4] Philippians 1:6.
[5] 1 Corinthians 16:14; Ephesians 5:2.

August 2

My love:
You are forgetting my love for you.
When you forget how much,
how great is my love for you,[1]
then you are vulnerable to fear.[2]
So think about my love.
Think about me "(rejoicing) over you with singing."[3]
Think about me having sacrificed my Son for you.[4]
Remember that I have only your best interests at heart.[5] Whatever
I do in your life, I do to bless you.[6]
So trust me.
I am with you.[7]
I will protect you from evil.[8]
Your reputation is in my hands, so do not fear.
"Be still, and know that I am God."[9]

---

[1] Psalm 108:4.
[2] 1 John 4:18.
[3] Zephaniah 3:17 (NIV).
[4] John 3:16; Romans 5:8; Romans 8:32.
[5] Jeremiah 29:11.
[6] Deuteronomy 28:1-14; Psalm 21:6.
[7] Matthew 28:20b.
[8] Psalm 23:4; Psalm 121:7; 2 Thessalonians 3:3.
[9] Psalm 46:10a (ESV).

August 3

My treasure, my love:
I am holding you close to my heart.[1]
It seems to you that I am waiting too long
to give you affirmative answers to your prayers.
Abraham thought the same thing![2]
I am not waiting longer than necessary.
I am working all things out in the best way possible.[3]
Trust me to provide the very best for you.[4]
Choose to be confident in my goodness.[5]
Choose to be confident in my generous and timely provision.
Choose to rest in me.[6]

---

[1] Psalm 17:8; John 1:18 (NLT).
[2] God promised Abraham that his descendants would be as numerous as the stars (Genesis 15:1-5) but Abraham had to wait until he was 100 years old before his first child was born (Genesis 21:1-7).
[3] Romans 8:28.
[4] Philippians 4:19.
[5] Psalm 27:13.
[6] Hebrews 4:9-10.

August 4

My treasure:
You are the apple of my eye![1]
Choose to believe
that I am looking after everything for you.[2]
Choose to believe
that you really can have confidence in me.[3]
Regardless of what you do or don't do,
I love you with an everlasting love
and you can afford to abandon yourself
and all you hold dear
into my care.[4]
Turn your back on worry and fear
and run towards me with hilarious confidence.
Not that you have far to run!
I am always with you,[5]
doting on you
and singing happy songs over you.[6]

---

[1] Psalm 17:8; Zechariah 2:8; Deuteronomy 32:10.
[2] Psalm 138:8 (NLT).
[3] Psalm 71:5; Proverbs 3:26; Hebrews 13:6.
[4] Psalm 55:22; 1 Peter 5:7.
[5] Matthew 28:20b.
[6] Zephaniah 3:17.

August 5

Dear friend,
today I will speak to you about faith.
Your faith can be as strong as I am
for it is in me that you place your confidence.
Remember this:
The effectiveness of faith
is determined by that on which the faith is placed.
Am I not completely trustworthy,[1]
all-powerful,[2]
and full of love and compassion?[3]
Do I not have the power and the will
to keep my Word?[4]
Do not see your faith as some puny, ineffectual thing,
for even a tiny mustard seed of faith in me
can move a mountain[5] –
because it is faith in **me**.
Do not focus on your faith;
focus on that on which you base your faith.
Do not have faith in your faith;
have faith in me.

---

[1] Psalm 145:13b (NIV).
[2] Psalm 89:8.
[3] Psalm 103:4.
[4] Jeremiah 1:12.
[5] Matthew 17:20.

August 6

My treasure:
"Do not let your heart be troubled…,"[1]
not even for one second.
I am in the midst of this situation.[2]
My Spirit is hovering over the face of this "deep,"[3]
brooding, creating, and bringing about change.
You cannot protect people
from the pain of their circumstances,
so don't try to do so.
Leave them in my hands.
My lovely:
Go to bed. Sleep.
I provide for you while you sleep.[4]

---

[1] John 14:1a (NASB).
[2] Isaiah 41:10; Isaiah 43:2.
[3] Genesis 1:2.
[4] Psalm 127:2b (NASB).

August 7

Treasure:
· Let me sing to you a song of love,
of love for my beloved.[1]
My treasure, my lovely:
I hold you in the palm of my hand,[2]
near to my heart.[3]
With my other hand,
I arrange circumstances for you.[4]
Nothing is happenstance.
Everything is ordained.
My love, my delight:
Day in and day out
I am whispering my plans
into your heart and mind.[5]
So lift your head, my child,
and proceed with confidence.
My treasure, my joy:
You are right to think
that there is something more in my plan for your life.[6]
I will bring it to pass.
Simply follow the promptings of my Spirit
and the desires in your heart.
My treasure, my dove:
You are right to think of every event as an opportunity
to build my Kingdom and to see my glory revealed.[7]
So be ready.
Be ready, my child, to speak my word in every circumstance.

---

[1] Isaiah 5:1; Zephaniah 3:17 (NLT).
[2] Isaiah 49:2; Isaiah 51:16; Isaiah 62:3.
[3] John 1:18 (NLT).
[4] Psalm 139:16; Ephesians 2:10.
[5] Psalm 138:8 (NLT); Philippians 2:13; John 16:13-14.
[6] Jeremiah 29:11.
[7] John 9:3; John 11:40.

August 8

My treasure:

Yes, it has been audacious of you

to question how I respond to your prayers.

Yes, of course, I forgive you.[1]

Yes, it has caused you great grief.

And yes! You can repent.[2]

I will give you the grace to repent.[3]

So pray, my child.

Lift up your heart,

Lift up your voice and pray.

Intercede for the saints.[4]

Intercede for the lost.[5]

Pray believing for me to act,[6]

and leave the ways and means to me –

and the timing as well.

My delightful child:

Do not be condemned by this.[7]

Receive my forgiveness and move on.

You have learned and relearned

the futility and foolishness

of questioning my ways and my timing.

Don't go there.

Pray and wait.[8]

---

[1] Psalm 86:5; 1 John 1:9.
[2] Joel 2:12-13; Acts 3:19-20.
[3] James 4:6; John 1:16.
[4] Ephesians 6:18.
[5] 1 Timothy 2:1.
[6] Matthew 21:22.
[7] Romans 8:1; John 12:47.
[8] Psalm 5:3.

Wait expectantly,
knowing that the gestation period for some prayers
is a very long time.
Do not be dismayed by apparent setbacks.
These may be needed for a greater good.
"(Keep your eyes on) Jesus,
the author and the finisher of (your) faith."[1]
My love:
You truly can have hilarious confidence in me.[2]
Walk into this day with joy and enthusiasm,
for I am your God!

---

[1] Hebrews 12:2a (NHEB).
[2] Psalm 71:5; Proverbs 3:26; Hebrews 13:6.

August 9

My treasure:
When your back is to the wind,
it is easy to get buffeted here and there,
but when you face the wind,
you can stay a course
and rise above your circumstances.
Put your hand in mine,
face this wind,
and march to victory.[1]

---

[1] James 1:2-8.

August 10

My treasure:
I am in the eye of your storm.
I am your peace and calm in the midst of turmoil.[1]
So be at rest.[2]
Let me permeate your being and your life.[3]
Let me be Lord of all.[4]
There is no need for any worry or anxiety or distress.[5]
I am Lord.
So breathe deeply and relax.
Relax, my love.
"Be still, and know that I am God."[6]

---

[1] John 14:27.
[2] Matthew 11:28-29.
[3] John 14:23; 1 John 4:16.
[4] Matthew 28:18.
[5] Isaiah 41:10.
[6] Psalm 46:10a (ESV).

August 11

My treasure, my love:

I love you with an everlasting love.[1]

I never will let you go.

Never.

You are mine.[2]

I bought you with a price[3]

and I never will let you go.[4]

Now, as for this mistake you think you made:

I will bring good out of it for you.[5]

You will see.

I already have brought good out of it for you.

So don't let your heart be troubled.

Believe in me.[6]

I am leading you. I am guiding you.[7]

Do not doubt this for one second.

My love for you is immense.[8]

My love for you is so immense, it consumes you:

You become lost in the immensity of it.

It is ridiculous to think that anything

could separate you from my love.

Nothing has the power to do that.

Nothing in heaven or earth.[9]

---

[1] Psalm 136; Psalm 103:17; Jeremiah 31:3.
[2] Isaiah 43:1.
[3] 1 Corinthians 6:20; 1 Corinthians 7:23.
[4] Hebrews 13:5b (WNT).
[5] Romans 8:28.
[6] John 14:1.
[7] Psalm 32:8 (NLT).
[8] Psalm 36:5; Psalm 103:11; Ephesians 3:17b-19.
[9] Romans 8:38-39.

Certainly not anything that you have done!
So let me gather you in my arms and comfort you.[1]
Let my love melt away your fears.[2]
Let my love permeate your entire being,
past and present and future.[3]
Let yourself be healed and soothed,
my treasure, my love.

---

[1] 2 Corinthians 1:3-4.
[2] Zephaniah 3:17 (NLT).
[3] John 14:23; 1 John 4:16.

August 12

My treasure, my love,
You can't worship both God and money.[1]
You have been too concerned about money.
It's only money –
a means to an end, not an end in itself.
You've been very concerned
about whether you'll have enough money
when I have told you not to worry
about food or clothes and so on.[2]
I am your God.[3] I am your Provider.[4]
Jehovah Jireh, that's who I am.[5]
Keep your eyes on this truth
and you'll be just fine.

---

[1] Matthew 6:24.
[2] Matthew 6:25.
[3] Ezekiel 34:31.
[4] Psalm 23.
[5] Genesis 22:14 (YLT).

August 13

My treasure, my lovely one:
Learn to be still in all situations[1] -
even, and especially, in situations
where things appear to go wrong.
There is so much you do not know and cannot know.
Trust that my Spirit is within you,
causing you to will and to do my purpose.[2]
Remember that these ones you care for are mine.
I have created them and I am saving them.[3]
They are my responsibility, not yours.
What has happened is an important step in my plan for them. Do
not try to rescue them from their pain
because I am using their pain to motivate them
to make the changes they need to make.
Sometimes, in my using you to effect my purposes,
you will get wounded.
You will bear the brunt of other's pain and anger and anguish.
Cling to me to be strengthened and healed and encouraged.[4]
My treasure, do not be condemned.[5]
Learn to live with the tension of unresolved issues.
When the time is right, I will show you what to do next.
As for the rest of today:
Lift up your head and smile and relax
and enjoy this day I have made for you.

---

[1] Zechariah 2:13; Psalm 131.
[2] Philippians 2:13.
[3] Titus 2:11 (NLT).
[4] Isaiah 40:29-31; Isaiah 41:10; Matthew 11:28-29.
[5] Romans 8:1.

August 14

My treasure, my love:
By all means, come to me with chutzpah![1]
I love it
when my kids are enthusiastic and insistent
in their prayers.
You can be that way
not because of your accomplishments,
but because of Jesus' work on the cross.
Thanks to Jesus' sacrifice,
you stand in my presence,
holy and blameless.[2]
So be bold!
Be nervy!
Be audacious!
Be insistent and enthusiastic!
Get very specific and lean in.

---

[1] Ephesians 3:12; Hebrews 4:16.
[2] Colossians 1:22.

August 15

My treasure, my love:
The truth
is that I have placed you in Christ[1]
who is very near to my heart.[2]
The only thing that changes
is your perception.
The reality
of your position in Christ
near to my heart
never changes.
Another truth
is that you are a magnificent creation of mine.[3]
Again, the only thing that changes
is your perception.
The reality
of the beauty and splendor of who you are
never changes.
Determine to believe the truth
and you will be set free.[4]

---

[1] 2 Corinthians 1:21.
[2] John 1:18 (NLT).
[3] Ephesians 2:10.
[4] John 8:32.

August 16

My treasure:
You are trying too hard.
You cannot do what only my Spirit can do.
You are just my instrument.[1]
So relax and let me flow through you.[2]
Relax and let me play music through you.
Relax and let me do it.
You try too hard.
"...my yoke is easy and my burden light."[3]
"Take my yoke...and learn from me,
for I am gentle and humble in heart
and you will find rest for your (soul)."[4]

---

[1] 2 Timothy 2:21; Acts 9:15.
[2] John 7:38-39.
[3] Matthew 11:30 (NIV).
[4] Matthew 11:29.

August 17

My treasure:
What joy to spend this time with you![1]
Think of it!
My Spirit entwined with yours,
permeating your body and soul.[2]
We are one, you and I.
So walk in that knowledge.
Know that I am causing you
to will and to do my pleasure.[3]
So lift up your heart and be happy!
I love you,
my treasure,[4] my precious child,[5] my love.

---

[1] Zephaniah 3:17; Psalm 149:4; John 15:11.
[2] John 14:23; 1 Corinthians 3:16; Romans 8:11; 1 John 4:16.
[3] Philippians 2:13.
[4] I Sam. 25:29 (NLT).
[5] 1 John 3:1; Romans 8:14-16; Galatians 3:26.

August 18

My precious child:
Look to me and live.[1]
I have placed you on the earth
at a specific time for a specific purpose
and I am bringing that to pass.[2]
Don't worry about a thing.
Expect me to work in and through you.[3]
Expect people to be transformed and healed.
My treasure, my lovely one:
Don't dwell on things that happened in the past and trouble you.
Hand them over to me and let them go.
There is no condemnation for you because you are in Jesus.[4]
Expect to be healed.
Expect to live long.
Expect to be a blessing.
Expect to be used by me to bless the earth.
My dearest:
I want you to know how very pleased I am with you.[5]
"(I am making) my face shine on you...
and (I) give you peace. [6]

---

[1] Isaiah 45:22.
[2] Psalm 138:8 (NLT); Ephesians 2:10.
[3] Philippians 2:13; Hebrews 13:21.
[4] Romans 8:1
[5] Zephaniah 3:17; Isaiah 62:4; Matthew 3:17.
[6] Numbers 6:24-25 (NASB).

August 19

Breathe deeply of my presence,[1] my love.
Breathe deeply of my love.[2]
There is nothing more valuable in life
than this oneness we experience.[3]
It is your food; it is your drink; it is your life.
My treasure,
open your heart to me and let me teach you.[4]
Embrace everything that happens in your life
with the assumption that there is something in it for you[5] -
even if your first response to it
is to recoil or resist or repel it.
As you do this,
you will discover the wisdom of this instruction.
My treasure;
I surround and fill you with my loving presence.
Go into this day with joy and enthusiasm
for you are in God
and God is in you.[6]

---

[1] Matthew 28:20b.
[2] 1 John 4:16.
[3] John 14:23; John 17:20-23; Revelation 3:20.
[4] Psalm 86:11; Matthew 11:29.
[5] Romans 8:28.
[6] John 14:23; John 15:11; 1 Corinthians 3:16; Romans 8:11; 2 Corinthians 4:7; 1 John 4:16; Revelation 3:20.

August 20

My treasure, my darling:
Just relax and be yourself.
I am your life[1]
and I am ordering all things in your existence.[2]
When things are not exactly as you would have them,
when your prayers are not answered
exactly as you would have them,
don't worry or fret.[3]
Instead, trust that I am involved
and that I know what I am doing.
So stop resisting.
Be who you are: weaknesses and all.
I work through your weaknesses
as well as your strengths.
My treasure:
Become aware of my love
enveloping you and permeating your being
to the core and to the extremities.[4]
I love you.[5]
Be strong in my love for you
and go into your day in the strength of that love.
"Be still, and know that I am God."[6]

---

[1] Job 33:4; Galatians 2:20.
[2] Psalm 138:8 (NLT).
[3] Matthew 6:25-34.
[4] Ephesians 3:16-19.
[5] Zephaniah 3:17; John 3:16; 1 John 4:16.
[6] Psalm 46:10a (ESV).

August 21

My treasure:

I love you.[1]

I love you with an everlasting love.[2]

Bask in my love for you.

Let it be your foundation, your life, your motivation,[3] your all.

As we grow in intimacy, you will become love;

when you and I are fully one, we will be one in love.

Whatever is not of love, is not of me.

Worry is not of love and thus is not of me.

Fear is not of love[4] and thus is not of me.

Jealousy is not of love and thus is not of me.

Impatience is not of love and thus is not of me.

Seek to remain in my love[5]

and live out of my love

and become my love.[6]

---

[1] Jeremiah 31:3; John 3:16; 1 John 4:16.
[2] Jeremiah 31:3.
[3] 1 Corinthians 16:14; Ephesians 5:2.
[4] 1 John 4:18.
[5] John 15:9.
[6] 1 John 4:16.

August 22

You are wondering about your work performance.
Let me take your face in my hands
and kiss each cheek
to thank you for what you do for me in your work.[1]
Yes, and let me give you a big hug!
As you and I grow in intimacy,
what you do will become increasingly more effective.
So don't let your heart be troubled
by any thoughts of inadequate performance,
My treasure, my love.

---

[1] Matthew 25:31-40.

August 23

My treasure, my love:
"Be still, and know that I am God."[1]
Trust that I am at work within you,
causing you to think my thoughts
and speak my words
and walk in my ways.[2]
I want you to dream,
to dream dreams of what you would like to happen
and then to believe
that I will cause these dreams to become reality.
You are my child,[3] created in my image,[4]
and I have placed my Spirit within you,[5] so dream.
Dream big dreams.
Dream bold dreams.
Speak it the way you want it to be and then wait.
Wait expectantly.
Wait with joy.
This is how I build my Kingdom, my treasure, my love:
My children dream dreams and I bring them to pass.
So: What are the dreams you will dream?
What are the desires of your heart?
What do you want me to create?
Let's build my Kingdom.
Don't be bound by what is.
Don't even be bound by what's possible.
No. Dream it the way you want it, because with me,
all things are possible.[6]

---

[1] Psalm 46:10a (ESV).
[2] Philippians 2:13.
[3] John 1:12; Romans 8:16; Galatians 3:26.
[4] Genesis 1:27.
[5] Ezekiel 36:27; 1 Corinthians 3:16.
[6] Jeremiah 32:17; Mark 10:27.

August 24

My treasure:
Nothing of importance has changed.
You are still in me and I am still in you.[1]
My love for you remains constant.[2]
When you commit to a plan,
you can expect your resolve to be tested.
Do not be thrown off course by this.
Continue to keep your eyes on Jesus and your goal[3]
and trust me to accomplish it for you.[4]

[1] Galatians 2:20; Romans 8:10; Colossians 3:3; 1 John 4:16.
[2] Micah 7:18.
[3] Proverbs 4:25; Hebrews 12:2.
[4] Psalm 37:5.

August 25

You are wondering
what I could possibly want to say to you
that I haven't already said.
Listen and find out!
You have been wondering
how I draw my children
into vibrant relationships with me.
Each journey is quite unique, my love.
The process begins long before the moment of conception
and continues into eternity.
The plan for each life includes infinite possibilities
because I honor free will.
The fingers of the wind of my Spirit
play exquisite music on the strings of each life.
Your prayers influence the development
of the songs being played
in the lives of the people you know.
Listen for the music, my love.

August 26

My treasure:
You **are** my treasure.[1]
I have made you my treasure.
That's the way it is
and that's the way it will be.
Today is the first day of the rest of your life.
Let's enjoy it together, you and I.
Do not be afraid.
Allow yourself to explore new areas.
Remember:
I have created all things
for my purpose and for my glory.[2]
Many, many people use what I have created
without acknowledging me – this is not new.
You, however, will give me the glory.
So proceed.
Have fun with this.
Yes, have fun!
Be carefree!
You can afford to
because I, the Almighty,
am your God.[3]

---

[1] Malachi 3:17 (NLT); Psalm 135:4 (NLT).
[2] Romans 11:36; Colossians 1:16.
[3] Ezekiel 34:31 (NLT); Isaiah 41:10.

August 27

My treasure, my love:
You have a ton of faith and you just don't know it!
You have enough faith to move several mountains![1]
Let's take a look at some people of faith:
The woman who touched the hem of my garment.[2]
The father of the demon-possessed child.[3]
The woman who asked for the crumbs that fell from the table.[4]
They were desperate.
They wouldn't take "No" for an answer.
They were prepared to pay any price.
How desperate are you?
How determined are you?
What price are you prepared to pay?

---

[1] Mark 11:23.
[2] Matthew 9:20-22.
[3] Matthew 17:14-21.
[4] Matthew 15:21-28.

August 28

My treasure, my love:
You can let this go.
You have suffered long enough with this pain.
Gather together all this pain
and bring it to the cross.
You will find
that my Son already has paid the price
for you to be free of this pain.[1]
Leave it there. Drop it. Let it go.
Forgive[2] and move on.
Reclaim your joy,[3] my love.
Reclaim that joy that I blessed you with
from the moment of conception.
Reclaim that excitement and wonder of life –
that delight in everything as it unfolds before you.
Reclaim that joy, my love.

---

[1] Isaiah 53:4.
[2] Luke 17:3-4.
[3] Isaiah 61:10 (NLT); John 15:9-11; Philippians 4:4.

August 29

My precious child:
I am your life.[1]
There is no one who has life
apart from my life.[2]
The world is divided
into those who know I have given them life
and those who don't know this truth.
There is no life apart from me.
Life is mine to give as I ordain.
Life is mine to take as I ordain.
All life is to be respected because I am the life.[3]
I am more than the life.
I am the Source of the life.[4]
I am the One who creates all
and breathes life into all.[5]

---

[1] John 11:25; Galatians 2:20; Colossians 3:4.
[2] Deuteronomy 32:39; Nehemiah 9:6.
[3] John 14:6.
[4] John 1:3; Colossians 1:16; Revelation 4:11.
[5] Genesis 2:7; Acts 17:25.

August 30

My treasure:
You are the apple of my eye[1]
and don't you forget it!
Do you know that I am going ahead,
making a way for you?
Yes, I am planning all the details.[2]
You don't need to worry about anything.
You don't need to try to control anything either.
Let go, my love.
Let go and experience my providence.
My treasure, my lovely:
I will open the storehouse of heaven for you.[3]
Pray expectantly.[4]

[1] Psalm 17:8; Deuteronomy 32:10; Zechariah 2:8.
[2] Psalm 138:8 (NLT); Deuteronomy 31:8.
[3] Deuteronomy 28:12; Philippians 4:19.
[4] Psalm 5:3 (NLT).

August 31

My treasure, my treasure:
I am right there with you in this sorrow.[1]
Cry your tears
and I will gather them
and hold them close to my heart.[2]
Remember that your life is hidden in me[3]
where all is well.
Put on patience,[4] my love,
and surrender this circumstance into my care.

---

[1] Matthew 28:20b.
[2] Psalm 56:8 (NLT).
[3] Colossians 3:3.
[4] Colossians 3:12.

September

My treasure:

I am closer to you than your heart.

I know you better, more intimately, than you know yourself.[1]

If you follow those little nudges,

those gentle hints on what to do or not do,

you will live.

I mean, **really** live.

Live abundantly.

Live fully.

Live extravagantly.

Live to the fullness of my life within you.[2]

So I set before you today a choice

between obedience or disobedience,

life or death.[3]

Choose life.

Choose life over and over.

Learn obedience,[4] my child.

Learn to obey minute by minute as my Son did.[5]

---

[1] Psalm 139.
[2] Ephesians 3:19; Colossians 2:9-10.
[3] Deuteronomy 30:19-20
[4] Hebrews 5:8.
[5] Philippians 2:8.

September 2

My love:

Yes, it's true.

I love you as much as I love my Son.[1]

I am just as pleased to live in you as I was to live in him.

In fact, I am just as pleased with you as I am with him.[2]

My pleasure has nothing to do with your performance.

It has everything to do

with my joy and delight with who you are:

My child.[3]

My creation.[4]

My treasure.[5]

It has everything to do with who I am.

I am love.[6]

I love – unconditionally.[7]

I create – perfectly.[8]

So, be ecstatically happy about this!

Be set free by this!

---

[1] John 17:23.
[2] Matthew 3:17; Matthew 17:5.
[3] Galatians 4:7; 1 John 5:1.
[4] Genesis 1:27; Ephesians 2:10.
[5] 1 Samuel 25:29 (NLT).
[6] 1 John 4:16.
[7] Romans 5:8.
[8] Genesis 1:31; 1 Timothy 4:4.

September 3

My treasure:
You are strong and courageous because I am your life.[1]
The notions of being weak and powerless
are lies serving to immobilize you.
Resist these lies!
Affirm your strength and beauty and courage.
Remember that you are yoked with Jesus;[2]
he will pull the load.

---

[1] Job 33:4; Galatians 2:20, Colossians 3:4.
[2] Matthew 11:29-30.

September 4

My treasure, my love:
Listen to the desires I have placed in your heart.[1]
They lie buried amidst dashed hopes and unfulfilled dreams.
My desires for you are pure.
My desires for you are perfectly suited to you.
My desires for you are attainable.
My desires for you bring joy and satisfaction.

---

[1] Jeremiah 29:11; Jeremiah 31:33; Ezekiel 11:19; Hebrews 8:10; Hebrews 10:16; 2 Corinthians 3:3.

September 5

Beautiful friend:
Your assignment is to rise above this situation.
You are not to be embroiled in the things of this world.[1]
Put your hand in mine
and walk on this dark and stormy water.[2]
See yourself detached from this situation –
stepping on it.
Yes, it is under your feet.[3]
You have dominion over it.
Take authority over it and command it to desist.

---

[1] Matthew 6:25-34; 1 Corinthians 7:31.
[2] Matthew 14:22-32.
[3] Luke 10:19.

September 6

My treasure, my love:
What I am providing is very good.[1]
One day you will fully understand the whys and wherefores.
In the meantime, celebrate my goodness at all times.[2]
You truly can afford to rejoice in all circumstances
because I AM![3]
I AM, my love.
Surrender and you will find joy.[4]

---

[1] Psalm 85:12a; Matthew 7:11; James 1:17.
[2] Psalm 106:1; Psalm 135:3.
[3] Exodus 3:14.
[4] Psalm 119:143b (NLT).

September 7

My treasure:
I am so delighted to be your life today.[1]
Let's enjoy this day together.
You can draw on my strength,
my wisdom,
my knowledge,
my insight –
I will be all you need.[2]

---

[1] Job 33:4; Galatians 2:20, Colossians 3:4.
[2] 2 Corinthians 9:8.

September 8

My child, I wish to speak to you of my love for you.
Let me speak in your heart.
I love you with an everlasting love[1] –
it has no beginning and no end.
I love you unconditionally,
regardless of your behavior.[2]
I love you with an intensity
that permeates all space and distance –
you cannot escape my love.[3]
My love for you has no beginning and no end –
it will never cease.
My love is your life;
it is all that you ever will be.
Learn to lean on my love,
to bask in my love,
to count on my love,
to rejoice in my love,
to move in my love,
to walk in my love,
and to emanate my love.

---

[1] Jeremiah 31:3.
[2] Romans 5:7-8.
[3] Psalm 139.

September 9

My treasure, my love:

Yes.

When you let go of wanting approval[1]

and when you quit condemning yourself,[2]

then you are free to reach out in love.[3]

That's what I am doing –

reaching out in love.

I **am** love![4]

You are my child[5] and love is in your genes,

so reach out in love.

Always.

You can love someone

even if you don't appreciate that person's way of being.

All is well, my love.

---

[1] Proverbs 29:25.
[2] Romans 8:1.
[3] 1 Corinthians 16:14; Ephesians 5:2.
[4] 1 John 4:16.
[5] 1 John 3:1.

September 10

Treasure, let's talk about discernment.
You were discerning something in your spirit tonight.
You were troubled by it, so you can know that it was not of me.
If you were to give it a label, what would you name it?
Self-righteousness? Phariseeism?
That spirit has been wreaking havoc for a very long time.
What is the fruit of it?
My response to it was to feel anxious, guarded,
and to want to back away.
It did not create peace or unity or a sense of safety.
What would you say is the opposite
of self-righteousness or Phariseeism?
Humility, gentleness, meekness (knowing your need for God).
Exactly.
You can learn from this.
I am humble and gentle in heart.[1]
As my child,[2] you also are humble and gentle in heart.

---

[1] Matthew 11:29.
[2] 1 John 3:1.

September 11

My love, my treasure:
Take your place in my presence and never leave.[1]
Never leave my side.
Learn how to be there always.
Jesus has paid the price for this,[2] so be there.
Be there, my child!
I have so much I want to share with you!
So much to enjoy and experience with you!
So take your place. Do take it!!
Never leave my side.
In my presence there is everything you need:
Fullness of joy.[3]
Wisdom.[4]
All the gifts of the Spirit.[5]
Knowledge.[6]
Insight.[7]
Health.[8]
Wealth.[9]
Discernment.[10]
You name it!
Come to the feast, my treasure.
I have prepared it for you, my love, for you.[11]
Come, my lovely one. Come!

---

[1] Colossians 1:22; John 15:4; John 15:9-10.
[2] 2 Corinthians 5:18.
[3] Psalm 16:11.
[4] Romans 11:33.
[5] 1 Corinthians 12; Ephesians 4; Romans 12.
[6] Proverbs 2:1-5.
[7] Proverbs 8:14.
[8] Proverbs 3:7-8.
[9] Proverbs 8:18.
[10] Psalm 119:66.
[11] Psalm 23:5; Luke 13:29.

September 12

My love, my treasure:

A good time for you to experience joy would be right now.

A good time for you to experience peace would be right now.

It is my will for you to be full of joy and peace at all times![1]

I am looking after everything for you,

so why not be full of peace and joy?[2]

I seriously am looking after every detail in your life.

You can afford to relax and be happy!

---

[1] Romans 15:13.
[2] Psalm 138:8 (NLT); Matthew 6:25-34.

September 13

My treasure, my sweetheart:
My love for you is enormous.[1]
It envelops you and permeates you.
It gives life to your body
and energizes and revives your soul and spirit.
My treasure, my lovely:
I am so pleased with you.[2]
I delight in you.
I sing songs of love over you.[3]
I have such joy in you!
So enjoy this life and my love.
Live life to the full and be content.[4]

---

[1] Psalm 37:23 (NLT); Psalm 103:11 (NLT); Ephesians 3:16-19.
[2] Psalm 147:11; Psalm 149:4 (NLT).
[3] Zephaniah 3:17.
[4] 1 Timothy 6:6.

September 14

My child, my love:
Rest in my love.
You are trying too hard -
"...my yoke is easy and my burden is light."[1]
So relax, my treasure.
I am at work in this situation.[2]
My treasure:
Know that I am Lord, that I am Sovereign.[3]
Let go of the need to control.
Let go of the need to have results.
Let go of everything except your relationship with me.

---

[1] Matthew 11:30 (NIV).
[2] Romans 8:28.
[3] Isaiah 44:24; Isaiah 45:18.

September 15

My treasure:
I would like you to ask yourself
what you would really like to do.
I would like you to be very honest
as you answer that question.
There is the concept of being in your "zone" or "sweet spot."[1]
When does that happen for you?
What is happening when you sense
a flow,
a synergy,
a moving beyond your natural capabilities,
pure joy and contentment in what you are doing?
Let yourself be guided by that, my treasure, my love.
I love you with an everlasting love.[2]

---

[1] For a discussion of living life in your zone or sweet spot, read *Cure for the Common Life: Living in Your Sweet Spot* by Max Lucado (Thomas Nelson: 2011).
[2] Jeremiah 31:3.

September 16

My treasure:
I am closer than your heartbeat.
I am filling you through and through.[1]
I am perfecting you
so we can be one with each other
and with all my children.[2]
Enjoy this day with me, my love, and remember –
"...my yoke is easy and my burden is light."[3]
When you feel heavy,
it's a signal to let go of something you are carrying.
Let it go and let me be your all.
I am your Creator, Redeemer, Savior,
Provider, Lord, Friend, Counselor, Guide –
with me as your Shepherd,
you truly have **everything** you need.[4]

---

[1] Ephesians 5:18b; Acts 13:52.
[2] 2 Corinthians 3:18; John 17:20-23.
[3] Matthew 11:30 (NIV).
[4] Psalm 23:1.

September 17

My treasure:
With great joy and delight
we celebrate our oneness with you.[1]
You can laugh in response to any circumstance.
"Be still, and know that I am God."[2]
Be still, and know that I live in you.[3]
Be still, and know that you live in me.[4]
Be still and be at peace.
Be content.
Be at peace.
Be filled with joy.
Be suffused with love.
Be imbued with faith.
For I am your life,[5]
My treasure, my love, my joy, my delight!

---

[1] John 14:23; 1 John 4:16; Revelation 3:20; Zephaniah 3:17.
[2] Psalm 46:10a (ESV).
[3] Galatians 2:20; Romans 8:11; 1 Corinthians 3:16.
[4] Ephesians 2:6; 1 John 4:16.
[5] Job 33:4; Galatians 2:20, Colossians 3:4.

September 18

Come close, my love,
and let yourself be nurtured in my warm embrace.
The interesting thing about needs
is that you have to become aware of them,
and even to experience discomfort or pain
regarding unmet needs,
before you are motivated to take steps
to get those needs met.
I will be with you in your search for kindred spirits.
Let me help you find exactly those beautiful people
I have chosen to be in your life.

September 19

My treasure:
I hold all things in my hands.[1]
All things are a part of my plan and purpose,
including that which seems negative.[2]
Let it all go and lose yourself in me.[3]
Lose yourself in me.
Lose yourself in me and you will find yourself.

*Yes!
just started job at
Hermosa Bch. & lots of
same issues

His plan!*

---

[1] Colossians 1:16-17.
[2] Romans 8:28.
[3] John 15:1-17.

September 20

Treasure:
I want to tell you again
that I know the pain you experience
regarding your estrangement from this one you love.
I don't expect you to walk away from that pain
or to rise above it.
It is a fiery furnace, this pain,
and I'm right there in it with you.[1]
The flames are burning away everything that is not of me.
You will emerge from this kiln
a purified and exquisite vessel.
When you become aware of the fire, remember:
I am with you
and I am bringing good out of this for you.

---

[1] Daniel 3; Isaiah 43:2; Matthew 28:20b.

September 21

My child, my treasure:
Be still and know that I am leading you.[1]
Do not worry about a thing.[2]
Remember that your life is hidden in Christ:[3]
Any motorcycle ride
will involve Jesus as the operator of the cycle.
You will be perfectly safe, hidden in him.
My treasure:
Lift up you head and laugh![4]
Have fun with this life I have given you!
Take risks!
I am there to catch you should you fall.[5]

1st day zooming w/ students, very nervous

---

[1] Psalm 32:8 (NLT).
[2] Matthew 6:25-34; Philippians 4:6.
[3] Colossians 3:3.
[4] Proverbs 31:25 (NLT).
[5] Deuteronomy 32:11.

September 22

My treasure:
Let me enfold you in my arms.
Let me hold you close.[1]
You have nothing to fear, my love.[2]
Yesterday I motivated you to do what I wanted you to do
and you did it.[3]
So relax.
I have engraved you in the palm of my hand.[4]
We are so close, you and I –
I in you; you in me.[5]
This is in response to my Son's prayer for unity.[6]
So you have nothing to fear.
I am looking after things for you.
"Be still, and know that I am God."[7]
Be still, my child, be still.

---

[1] Psalm 91:4; Psalm 17:8.
[2] Jeremiah 17:7-8; Micah 4:4.
[3] Philippians 2:13.
[4] Isaiah 49:2; Isaiah 51:16 (NLT).
[5] John 14:23; 1 John 4:15; Revelation 3:20.
[6] John 17:20-23.
[7] Psalm 46:10a (ESV).

September 23

My treasure, my love:
Breathe deeply of my love.[1]
Breathe deeply of my life.[2]
Breathe deeply of my energy to sustain and heal you.[3]
And remember:
I am at work in you,
causing you to will and to do my pleasure.[4]
You can depend on it.
So relax and enjoy each day as it unfolds.

---

[1] 1 John 4:16
[2] Genesis 2:7; Job 33:4; Acts 17:25.
[3] Psalm 55:22; Isaiah 46:4; Psalm 41:3.
[4] Philippians 2:13.

September 24

My treasure, my love:
Your tears are my tears.
Your burden is my burden.
We carry it together, my love.[1]
Let my life sustain you, rejuvenate you.[2]
Let my joy lift you up.[3]

---

[1] Matthew 11:28-30; 2 Corinthians 1:5; 1 Corinthians 6:19.
[2] Philippians 4:13.
[3] Nehemiah 8:10b.

September 25

My treasure:
Listen to what's in your heart.[1]
I speak from that central space.
That's where you and I commune.
That's where I show you what I am saying and doing.[2]
My child, I have so much I wish to share with you.
It requires that you still and quiet your soul[3]
to listen to my Spirit.[4]

---

[1] Ezekiel 3:10; Psalm 40:8; Psalm 119:11.
[2] John 5:19; John 12:49.
[3] Psalm 131:2; Psalm 62:1.
[4] John 16:13; Acts 2:16-17.

September 26

My treasure:

"Be still, and know that I am God."[1]

My treasure:

I am in you.[2]

I am pleased to dwell in you in all my fullness.[3]

Be open to experiencing me live in and through you

in new and different ways.

My treasure:

Do not get upset about what is not happening.

Do not get stuck in a rut,

expecting me to do what I have done elsewhere

through other people.

It's a new day and I am doing a new thing.[4]

Be excited.

Be faithful.

Be patient.

Watch and see.

---

[1] Psalm 46:10a (ESV).
[2] John 14:23; 1 John 4:16; Revelation 3:20.
[3] Colossians 1:19; John 1:16; John 14:23.
[4] Isaiah 43:19.

September 27

My love, my treasure:
Lift up your heart and be glad
because I am your Sovereign![1]
I am at work in you,
cleansing you and shaping you into an instrument
perfect for my purpose and perfect for my pleasure.[2]
Don't worry about anything.
This is **my** work. The onus is on me.
Your part is to be obedient
to obey the promptings of my Holy Spirit.[3]
Remember:
"…my yoke is easy and my burden is light."[4]

---

[1] Ezekiel 34:31 (NLT).
[2] Philippians 1:6; 1 Corinthians 1:8; 1 Thessalonians 3:13; Philippians 2:13.
[3] John 16:13; Romans 8:9.
[4] Matthew 11:30 (NIV).

September 28

My child, my treasure:
Let my Word live in you.[1]
Dwell on it.
Dwell in it.
Let it speak life and healing and power to you.[2]
Let me talk to you about how this works:
When my Word is presented,
my Spirit is present there,
sorting through the message
and planting the right words
in the right heart
at the right time.
Do not underestimate
the power of my Word
to transform lives.[3]

---

[1] Colossians 3:16; Deuteronomy 11:18; Psalm 119:11.
[2] Hebrews 4:12 (NIV); Ephesians 6:17.
[3] Hebrews 4:12 (NIV); Luke 8:1-15.

September 29

My beautiful child:
I am so close to you
in this place of intimacy that we share![1]
Can you feel my heartbeat?
Lean your head up against my chest and listen.
Breathe deeply of my grace and mercy and love.
Your life is unfolding beautifully
according to my plan.[2]
Surrender to my heartbeat
and live life to the fullest.

---

[1] John 14:23; Revelation 3:20; Ephesians 2:6.
[2] Psalm 138:8 (NLT); Philippians 1:6; Psalm 139:16.

September 30

My treasure:
Yes, I did allow this to happen.
I am enabling you to learn
that your peace and joy
is not dependent on circumstances.
I am enabling you to learn
that when things happen
that do not meet your approval,
I still am God and my intention
is to bring good out of the circumstance.[1]
I am enabling you to learn
that my ways are above your ways.[2]
I am enabling you to learn
that my plan is to prosper you
and never to harm or deprive you.[3]
I am enabling you to learn
that sometimes those closest to you
will attack you.[4]
In all of this,
nothing will separate you from my love.[5]
And that's what's most important,
my treasure, my love.
I am making it possible
for you to be able to maintain your resolve
to positively expect me to do something good.[6]

---

[1] Romans 8:28.
[2] Isaiah 55:9.
[3] Jeremiah 29:11.
[4] Psalm 41:9; Psalm 55:12-14; Luke 22:21.
[5] Romans 8:38-39.
[6] Philippians 2:13.

October

October 1

My treasure, my love:
Rest in me.[1]
Find your comfort and your security in me.[2]
Be at peace,
knowing that I am in you and you are in me.[3]
My treasure, let yourself dream.[4]
Let yourself imagine what you would like to accomplish.
I will be present, guiding your imaginings.[5]
Dream big dreams,
my child, my friend, my partner,
because the harvest field is white.[6]

---

[1] Psalm 37:7a; Matthew 11: 28; Hebrews 4:9-10.
[2] Isaiah 66:13; 2 Corinthians 1:3-4.
[3] John 14:23; Revelation 3:20; Ephesians 2:6.
[4] Acts 2:17.
[5] Philippians 2:13.
[6] Luke 10:2.

October 2

My love:
It is not an accident
that you are who you are
or where you are
or that you are living when you are.
There is nothing about your life
that is accidental or unimportant or unnecessary.[1]
I am working out my purpose on this earth[2]
and for this I prepared you
and prepared a place for you.
Nothing about you is an accident:
your gender, your interests, your appearance, your aptitudes… All
is according to my design.
So take your place.
Stand tall and strong.
Throw away timidity and defensiveness.[3]
Be who you are,
enjoy who you are,
and enjoy a relationship with me
that is characterized by surrender[4] and empowerment.[5]
And give yourself permission to rest.
Take time off from your endeavors.
My love:
Stop thinking in terms of "I"
and start thinking in terms of "we"
because I live in you[6]
and we walk through life together.[7]

---

[1] Psalm 138:8 (NLT); Psalm 139:16b.
[2] Ephesians 1:11; Isaiah 46:9-10.
[3] 2 Timothy 1:7.
[4] Psalm 37:5; Proverbs 3:5; Galatians 5:25 (NLT).
[5] Ephesians 3:16; 2 Timothy 1:7.
[6] 1 Corinthians 3:16; John 14:23; Galatians 2:20.
[7] Matthew 11:29; Matthew 28:20b.

October 3

My treasure, my love:
Keep looking to me[1] and putting your hope in me.[2]
Keep trusting me to provide for your every need.[3]
Enter into my rest,[4]
knowing that I have accomplished it all.
Yes, indeed, I have accomplished it all.
It is done.
It is finished.
My will already has been accomplished.
You will see and you will marvel.
It's R & R for you, my love:
Resting and Rejoicing in my completed work on your behalf.

---

[1] Psalm 105:4.
[2] Psalm 131:3.
[3] Psalm 52:8.
[4] Hebrews 4:1-11; Matthew 11:28-30.

October 4

My treasure, my joy and delight:
You can trust that I am at work in you[1]
in **all** the circumstances of your life,
so relax and go with the flow of my mighty current –
the current that flows from my throne in heaven[2]
and from your heart.[3]
You will know what you need to do
and you will know what you need to not do.
So let it all go.
Relax.
Enjoy this life, this day, this minute.
I have given it to you to enjoy with me.

Thank you

---

[1] Philippians 2:13.
[2] Revelation 22:1.
[3] John 7:38.

October 5

Be still, my love.
Breathe deeply and be still.
All is well, my love, all is well.
You have nothing to fear, for my love surrounds you.[1]
There is no need to get upset about anything.
Look at me.[2]
Turn away from what troubles you and look at me.
See my greatness[3] and my goodness.[4]
Recognize my supremacy[5] and faithfulness.[6]
Put your concerns in my capable hands and let it all go.[7]
Relax, my child.
Yes, there is a "thief (who) comes to steal and kill and destroy."[8]
He does this by accusing,[9] deceiving[10] and tempting.[11]
But you overcome that enemy "by the blood of the Lamb
and the word of (your) testimony."[12]
Stand on what Jesus did for you,
resist the devil with scripture[13] and be happy.[14]
Be happy! I want you to be happy, my love.
Let my joy be your strength and bring wholeness to your body.[15]

---

[1] Isaiah 54:10.
[2] Hebrews 12:2.
[3] Psalm 70:4 (NLT); Psalm 77:13.
[4] Nahum 1:7; Psalm 135:3; 1 Peter 2:9 (NLT).
[5] Colossians 1:15-23.
[6] Lamentations 3:22-23.
[7] Philippians 4:6.
[8] John 10:10a (NIV); 1 Peter 5:8.
[9] Zechariah 3:1; Job 1:6; Revelation 12:10.
[10] Revelation 12:9.
[11] Matthew 4:3.
[12] Revelation 12:11a (NIV).
[13] James 4:7; Matthew 4:1-11.
[14] 1 Thessalonians 5:16.
[15] Nehemiah 8:10; Malachi 4:2.

October 6

My treasure, my love:
Look to me and live.[1]
I am your life, your all.[2]
And you are my treasure, my delight.[3]
Nothing can alter that reality.
Rest in this existence.
Nothing else matters.
My love, my treasure, my delight.
"Be still, and know that I am God."[4]
Be still.
Relax.
Smile.
Breathe deeply.
Live in the flow of my life within you.[5]
Look for my life in all you meet.
Call on that life.
Call it into being.
Call it into being lived.
And laugh,[6] my child.
Laugh uproariously
because Jesus Christ is the Lord of **All,**[7]
My treasure, my love.

---

[1] Psalm 105:4; Isaiah 45:22 (NLT).
[2] Job 33:4; Galatians 2:20, Colossians 3:4.
[3] Malachi 3:17 (NLT); Psalm 135:4 (NLT); Zephaniah 3:17.
[4] Psalm 46:10a (ESV).
[5] John 4:14; John 7:38-39.
[6] Proverbs 31:25 (NLT).
[7] Acts 10:36; Matthew 28:18; Romans 10:12.

October 7

My treasure, my love:
I am filling you with my love for today.[1]
Let it permeate your being.
Let it soothe your jangled nerves.
Let it bring peace to your body, soul, and spirit.[2]
Let it flow out to all you meet.[3]
Let it be your guide and motivation.[4]
I am love.[5]
You are created in my image,[6]
so you are love.
Be that love today.

---

[1] John 15:9; Jude 1:1-2; 1 John 4:16.
[2] Zephaniah 3:17.
[3] John 4:14; John 7:38-39.
[4] 1 Corinthians 16:14; Ephesians 5:2.
[5] 1 John 4:16.
[6] Genesis 1:26-27.

October 8

My love, I set this up for you.
Just like I led Abraham up the mountain to sacrifice Isaac[1]
so that Abraham could see what was in his heart,
so I led you up this mountain
to help you see what is in your heart –
your tendency to fear others,
to be guided by what you think others may be thinking.
This is a false god.
I am a jealous God[2] –
I would have you worship me alone
because I alone am able to provide for you and protect you.[3]
It is only when you worship me that your needs will be met.
You may think that others have power over you,
but they have no power except that I give it to them.[4]
So it is I who am in control.
All power is mine.[5]
I dispense it as I please
and all are accountable to me for how they use it.[6]
The big picture, my treasure, is one in which Jesus is Lord.[7]
I have given him all power and authority
and he dispenses it at will.[8]
Everything is under his jurisdiction.[9]

---

[1] Genesis 22:1-18.
[2] Exodus 34:14.
[3] Isaiah 46:4 (NLT); Philippians 4:19.
[4] John 19:11.
[5] Nehemiah 9:6; Matthew 28:18.
[6] Hebrews 13:17 (NLT); Romans 12:14.
[7] Acts 10:36; Matthew 28:18; Romans 10:12.
[8] Matthew 28:18; Colossians 2:10.
[9] Hebrews 1:3; Colossians 1:17.

Jesus is Lord.
You have nothing to fear.
Your fear comes from seeing others as Lord.
This is a "false pretension
that sets itself up against the knowledge of God."[1]
This is a stronghold in your mind
that needs to be demolished.
You will demolish it with truth.[2]

---

[1] 2 Corinthians 10:5a (NIV).
[2] John 8:32.

October 9

My treasure,
Store this image in your heart
because it is a true picture:
I am a strong warrior[1]
and I am standing at your side.
This battle is mine, not yours.[2]
This battle is mine, not yours.
My dearly beloved child,
you have nothing to fear.
I am your strong protector.[3]
So relax.
Enjoy this day I have given you.
"Be still, and know that I am God."[4]

---

[1] Jeremiah 20:11 (NLT); 1 Kings 22:19 (NLT); Isaiah 37:16 (NLT); Romans 8:31.
[2] 2 Chronicles 20:15; 1 Samuel 17:47 (NLT).
[3] Psalm 62:7; 2 Samuel 22:32-33.
[4] Psalm 46:10a (ESV).

October 10

My treasure, my love:

I am living in you.[1]

You have no idea how much of what you do is actually me.

Occasionally, you step out on your own.

Know that I am at work in you,

causing you to do my will.[2]

I am your Lord.[3]

Learn to affirm yourself.

Fill your mind with positive thoughts.[4]

---

[1] Revelation 3:20; John 14:23.
[2] Philippians 2:13.
[3] Isaiah 48:17; Joel 2:27; 2 Thessalonians 1:12 (NLT).
[4] Philippians 4:8.

October 11

My treasure, my love:
I am surrounding and filling you with my love.[1]
Relax and receive my healing presence.
Jesus could sleep in the boat
because he knew my presence.[2]
He knew my indwelling and surrounding love –
that perfect love in which there is no fear.[3]
He also knew that I would rescue him
whenever he got in trouble.[4]
And he got into trouble all the time!
My treasure:
You have nothing to fear,
because I always am with you.[5]
I am guiding the process.[6]
I am keeping it safe for you.
Because I am here, in and around you,
no evil can come near.[7]

---

[1] John 15:9; Jude 1:1-2; 1 John 4:16.
[2] Mark 4:35-41.
[3] 1 John 4:18.
[4] Psalm 91; 2 Timothy 4:18.
[5] Matthew 28:20b.
[6] Psalm 32:8 (NLT); Psalm 138:8 (NLT).
[7] Psalm 121:7; 2 Thessalonians 3:3.

October 12

My love:

I see your heart.

I know your heart.[1]

I know what I have placed there.[2]

Give yourself permission to dream.

Just do it.

Don't be afraid, because I love you deeply.[3]

Be at peace,[4] take heart, and be strong.[5]

Don't wait for someone else to do this thing you are carrying.

Birth it yourself.

Just do it.

Do it with joy and enthusiasm.

Expect me to provide whatever you need when you need it.[6]

Let yourself run with this.

Throw caution to the wind – I will pick up the pieces!

My treasure, my love:

Let yourself be motivated by compassion,[7]

and by faith in the power of my Word.[8]

---

[1] 1 Chronicles 28:9; 1 Samuel 16:7; 1 Kings 8:39.
[2] Philippians 2:13.
[3] 1 John 4:16.
[4] John 14:27; 2 Thessalonians 3:16.
[5] Psalm 27:14; Psalm 31:24; John 16:33.
[6] Philippians 4:19; 2 |Corinthians 9:8.
[7] Matthew 14:14; Mark 6:34; Luke 7:12-15; 2 Corinthians 16:14.
[8] Isaiah 55:11; Hebrews 4:12; Matthew 24:35.

October 13

My treasure:

Stop worrying.[1]

Start rejoicing.[2]

I am doing great and mighty things.[3]

Stop looking for approval from others:

this is notoriously unreliable:[4]

Sometimes people disapprove while I approve.

Sometimes people approve while I disapprove.

So just don't go there.

Continue to lean on me

and trust me to be at work in and through you.[5]

---

[1] Matthew 6:25-34; Philippians 4:6.
[2] 1 Thessalonians 5:16.
[3] Deuteronomy 3:24 (NLT).
[4] Proverbs 29:25; Matthew 22:16; John 2:24 (NLT).
[5] Philippians 2:13.

October 14

My treasure, my love:
Receive this piece of truth that will set you free:[1]
When you give in
to the temptation to experience condemnation,
the fruit of it is fear and separation from me.
You have been tormented by this for a very long time,
but no more!
Use your sword[2] to get victory over this temptation.
"There is…no condemnation (whatsoever)
for those who are in Christ Jesus"[3]

---

[1] John 8:32.
[2] Ephesians 6:17.
[3] Romans 8:1 (ESV).

October 15

Dear friend:
I am so pleased to live in you![1]
I have washed you clean[2]
and we stand in God's presence,
holy and blameless, without a single fault.[3]
So lift up your head.
Stand tall and strong.
And relax.
You are wondering what to do with all the pain you encounter. Do
what I did with it when I walked on this earth:
I lifted it up to my Father.
I did not carry those sins and sicknesses and sorrows
until the time when I was asked to go to the cross.
So cast these cares on God,[4]
or put them on my cross[5] –
whatever suits you.
The reason my yoke is easy and my burden is light[6]
is because I already have done the work on the cross
for all of time.[7]
I am asking you to love the people I send to you
by giving them quality time and by praying for them.
And so:
Go and enjoy this day that I have made for you![8]

---

[1] 1 Corinthians 3:16; 1 Corinthians 6:19; John 14:23.
[2] 1 Corinthians 6:11; Ephesians 5:26.
[3] Colossians 1:22 (NLT).
[4] Psalm 55:22; 1 Peter 5:7.
[5] Isaiah 53:4-5.
[6] Matthew 11:30.
[7] Romans 6:10; Hebrews 10:10.
[8] Psalm 118:24.

October 16

Dear friend:
When I lived in the flesh,
my one aim was to serve my Father
by serving those I loved.[1]
Open your heart to receive my love
for those I have placed in your life,
and you will be freed to serve.
Do this willingly and do it graciously,
for I am pouring out abundant blessing through you.[2]
Dear one –
hold this truth in your heart,
ponder it, never lose sight of it,
for I am love[3] and came to serve.[4]
To this end I commission you.
Go in my authority and my power and never look back!

---

[1] Mark 10:45.
[2] John 7:38.
[3] 1 John 4:16.
[4] John 13:1-17; Philippians 2:6-8.

October 17

My treasure:
Let it all go.
Let everything go.
Cling to me alone.[1]
When you let it all go,
you will be free to find me.[2]
When you have stilled and quieted your soul,
you will be able to perceive my presence.[3]

---

[1] Psalm 63:8.
[2] Matthew 16:24-26.
[3] Psalm 131.

October 18

My treasure:
Choose life.[1]
Be confident that I am within you
choosing life and causing you to choose life.[2]
Choosing life is choosing my character and my presence.
It is choosing my glory.
Choose to reflect my glory in every area of your life.

My treasure, you are worrying.
Even though you have asked me to be Lord of this area,
you are worrying!
Choose to believe that I am being faithful
and cut off the worrying.[3]
Worrying has no place in your new life in Christ.[4]
Seriously!
You have enough faith to move a mountain![5]

---

[1] Deuteronomy 30:19.
[2] Philippians 2:13; Galatians 2:20.
[3] Philippians 4:6-7; Ephesians 4:22.
[4] Colossians 3:1; 2 Corinthians 5:17; 1 Peter 2:24.
[5] Mark 11:23.

October 19

My treasure, my love:
Enter into my rest.[1]
Do your best,
in the power of my Spirit,
and then let it go.
Leave the results to me.[2]
Leave the judging to me.[3]
I am not holding you responsible for the results.
My treasure:
I see your heart –
your sincere desire to please me.
Offer your works up to me as a sacrifice of praise[4]
and wait to see what I will do.
Always trust, always hope, always believe.[5]

---

[1] Hebrews 4:1-11; Matthew 11:28-30.
[2] Isaiah 49:4.
[3] 2 Timothy 4:1; Romans 2:16; Acts 10:42 (NLT).
[4] Hebrews 13:15-16.
[5] 1 Corinthians 13:7; Romans 15:13; Psalm 52:8 (NLT).

October 20

My treasure, my love:
Just as my Son and I are one,[1]
so also are you one with us.
It is just as Jesus prayed:
"I in them and you in me."[2]
There is no longer a separate existence, an independence.
We are one –
a union resulting in a new creation,
a new creature.[3]
The old nature[4] is like the by-products or waste matter
following the process of production.
Ignore it. It is of no importance.
You are a brand new creation in Christ.[5]

---

[1] John 10:30.
[2] John 17:21 (NIV).
[3] 2 Corinthians 5:17.
[4] Romans 6:6; Romans 7:5 (NLT); Ephesians 4:22 (NLT); Colossians 3:9.
[5] 2 Corinthians 5:17.

October 21

My treasure, my love:
I am within you,[1]
causing you to will and to do my pleasure.[2]
I am leading you and guiding you.[3]
I am building my Kingdom through you.
When you speak, I am speaking.
When you pray, I am praying.
When you serve, I am serving.
We live and move in sync, you and I.
Your new nature is just like me.[4]
Keep taking off the grave clothes that bind you,[5] my love,
until you are completely free
to live and move and have your being in me.[6]

---

[1] John 14:23; 1 John 4:16; Revelation 3:20.
[2] Philippians 2:13.
[3] Psalm 32:8 (NLT).
[4] Ephesians 4:24.
[5] John 11:44; Ephesians 4:22; Colossians 3:9.
[6] Acts 17:28.

October 22

My treasure, my love:
I have been living within you for a very long time.[1]
We are old friends, you and I.
By now, pretty much whatever you feel like doing
is what I am doing.
So feel free.
Do what gives you pleasure.
Do it with enthusiasm and joy –
go for the gusto!
I have placed my desires in your heart,[2]
so forge ahead.
Be very courageous.[3]

---

[1] 1 Corinthians 3:16; 1 Corinthians 6:19; John 14:23; 1 John 4:16; Revelation 3:20.
[2] Ezekiel 36:26; Psalm 51:10; Jeremiah 24:7; 2 Corinthians 5:17.
[3] Joshua 1:7-9.

October 23

My child, my treasure:
"Be still, and know that I am God."[1]
Be still and enter into my presence.[2]
You will need to leave your old nature[3] behind –
All that guilt and condemnation
has no place in my presence.
Let it drop off.
In fact, shake it off![4]
It is glued to you through old neural pathways.
Replace those pathways with new thoughts
celebrating who you are in me.
Celebrate your new nature in Christ.[5]
Your true essence is to be joyful and serene.[6]
When you are not experiencing peace and joy,
you are adhering to your old nature.
Shut that down by choosing to be grateful
and to honor your identity in me.

---

[1] Psalm 46:10a (ESV).
[2] Colossians 1:22.
[3] Romans 6:6; Romans 7:5 (NLT); Ephesians 4:22 (NLT); Colossians 3:9.
[4] Romans 4:22-24.
[5] 2 Corinthians 5:17.
[6] Galatians 5:22-23.

October 24

My treasure:
I am allowing you
to experience the suffering of my children
so that you can birth the Word
I am speaking to them through you.
In this way
you are entering into or sharing my suffering[1]
and making the way of salvation and deliverance.
Rejoice, for I am yoked together with you in this endeavor.[2]
Relax about the process
because I am looking after each detail.
I am raising an army of wounded soldiers
who know my salvation,
who have tasted and know that my salvation is good.[3]
It is with these people,
with these children of mine,
that I will build my church;
for they, having experienced the depths of despair,
will not give up at the first sign of opposition or adversity.
It is not a bad thing to be wounded or crippled.
I use this to reveal my glory.[4]

---

[1] Colossians 1:24.
[2] Matthew 11:29-30.
[3] Psalm 34:8; 1 Peter 2:3.
[4] John 9:2-3; John 11:4,40.

October 25

My treasure, my dear child:
You are deeply troubled by your performance yesterday.
That is your old nature,[1] fretting and fussing.
Ignore it.
You are not obligated to pay any attention to it.
Treat it as grave clothes and let it drop off.[2]
It has nothing to do with your life in my Son.[3]
No matter what you're feeling,
your true reality is righteousness, peace, joy[4] and love.[5]
Jesus bought this for you by giving his life.[6]
So be done with self-condemnation and approval seeking –
it is irrelevant.
Just get on with celebrating your new life
of righteousness, peace, joy, and love.

---

[1] Romans 6:6; Romans 7:5 (NLT); Ephesians 4:22 (NLT); Colossians 3:9.
[2] Ephesians 4:22; Colossians 3:9.
[3] Colossians 3:1-4.
[4] Romans 14:17.
[5] 1 John 4:16.
[6] 1 John 3:16.

October 26

My treasure, my love:
Today is a beautiful new day I have created for you.[1]
Leave all your cares with me[2]
and enjoy it to the max.
You are my treasure.[3]
I carry you in my treasure pouch,[4]
and nothing else matters!

---

[1] Psalm 118:24.
[2] Philippians 4:6; 1 Peter 5:7.
[3] Exodus 19:5 (NLT); Song of Solomon 4:12 (NLT).
[4] I Sam. 25:29 (NLT).

October 27

My love, my treasure:
I am so pleased to dwell with you![1]
Do you know that every day
I am transforming you
into a true likeness of Jesus?[2]
I am quite happy to live in the messiness of your life.

---

[1] Zephaniah 3:17 (NLT); John 14:16-17; John 14:23; 1 John 4:16; Revelation 3:20.
[2] Romans 8:29; 2 Corinthians 3:18.

October 28

Beautiful friend:
I am with you
as you proceed on this challenging path.[1]
I am with you
as you consider what my being Lord means
when you experience the incomprehensible.
You are right in acknowledging that I am Lord
because of who I am.[2]
I am Lord
no matter how you evaluate what I do or don't do.
I am Lord of your life
no matter what happens.
Honoring me as Lord of your life
involves assertively addressing,
rather than passively accepting,
the challenges that surface.
Honoring me as Lord of your life
involves doing your best to trust and obey.[3]
Honoring me as Lord of your life
involves working together with me
to bring good out of every situation.[4]

---

[1] Isaiah 41:10; Isaiah 43:2; Matthew 28:20b.
[2] Isaiah 44:24.
[3] Psalm 78:7.
[4] Romans 8:28.

October 29

My love, my treasure:
Put your hope in me.[1]
Yes, absolutely!
I am completely trustworthy[2] and able
to manage all your cares and more.[3]
Put your hope in me and rest.[4]
Put your hope in me
and be filled with joy.[5]
Put your hope in me
and find yourself immersed in my love.[6]
All is well, my love.
All is well.

---

[1] Psalm 130:7; Psalm 131:3.
[2] Psalm 145:13 (NIV); Hebrews 10:23 (NIV).
[3] Romans 4:21; 2 Corinthians 9:8.
[4] Job 11:18 (NLT); Acts 2:26 (NLT).
[5] Romans 15:13; Acts 2:2
[6] Romans 5:5; Psalm 33:22.

October 30

My love, my treasure:
Today is a new day!
Enjoy this day and be very glad.[1]
You are mine and I am yours – [2]
It doesn't get better than that!
Yesterday is gone, tomorrow is not here –
today is what we have.
So let's really enjoy this day.
Walk through this day hand in hand with me.

---

[1] Psalm 118:24.
[2] Isaiah 43:1; Ezekiel 34:31.

October 31

My treasure, my love:
I am right there with you in this struggle.[1]
Let me hold you close to my heart.[2]
This challenge is not meant to harm you,
but to build your faith.[3]
It is an opportunity
to learn to have joy in all circumstances.[4]
I know what's coming in your life.[5]
..."I know the plans I have for you...
plans for good and not for disaster
to give you a future and a hope."[6]
Let me carry you through this time.[7]

---

[1] Isaiah 41:10; Isaiah 43:2; Matthew 28:20b.
[2] Psalm 63:8; Isaiah 40:11 (NLT).
[3] James 1:2-4; Romans 5:3-4.
[4] Philippians 4:4; 1 Thessalonians 5:16.
[5] Psalm 138:8 (NLT).
[6] Jeremiah 29:11 (NLT).
[7] Isaiah 46:4.

November

November 1

I want you to know, my treasure, my love,
that I am tremendously pleased with you![1]
I just think you are most special!
I wouldn't want you to be any different than you are![2]
Just keep on doing what you are doing and that will suit me fine!
I'm delighted with you, for sure.[3]
I also want you to know
that I am painstakingly "(guiding) you
along the best pathway for your life.
I (am advising) you and (watching) over you."[4]
Have fun exploring new areas
and watch to see what develops.
Nothing happens by accident, my love.
I'm organizing it all and working it all out for your good.[5]
You'll see.
Draw close to me and I'll draw close to you.[6]
Well, actually, you'll find that I already am close to you!
I am as close as your breath.[7]
So just enjoy our closeness
and live my love and my joy and my peace.
What I have is yours to enjoy.[8]
It's all yours to enjoy and to live.
Yes, live my life.[9]
Live my love, live my joy, live my peace.

---

[1] Zephaniah 3:17.
[2] Genesis 1:31.
[3] Zephaniah 3:17; Psalm 147:11 (NLT); Psalm 149:4.
[4] Psalm 32:8 (NLT).
[5] Romans 8:28; Psalm 138:8 (NLT).
[6] James 4:8a.
[7] John 14:23; Ephesians 3:16-17.
[8] Luke 15:31; Romans 8:17; Ephesians 3:6.
[9] Galatians 2:20.

November 2

My treasure:
How difficult it is for you to experience my peace
when you are thinking thoughts that create fear!
Why not think thoughts that create peace?
Think thoughts about my care for you.[1]
Think thoughts about my plans for you.[2]
Think thoughts about how I have kept you safe in times past.[3]
Think thoughts about how I have kept others safe –
like Daniel, for example.[4]
Or his friends, Shadrach, Meshach and Abednego.[5]
This fearing disaster is an old, old pattern
by which you have tormented yourself for many years.
When you surrender to this way of being,
you relegate me to the sidelines.
I recommend that you keep me front and center!
I recommend that you celebrate my love and care for you.
Pick your favorite song of my love and care
and sing it until the fear is replaced by peace.

---

[1] Luke 12:28; 1 Peter 5:7.
[2] Jeremiah 29:11.
[3] Psalm 71:6; Jude 1:1 (NLT).
[4] Daniel 6.
[5] Daniel 3.

November 3

My child, my love:
You are the apple of my eye![1]
I am so very pleased with you.[2]
Enter into my rest,[3]
accomplished for you
by the work of Jesus on the cross.
All this consternation you're experiencing –
that's your old nature.[4]
You are no longer obligated to pay attention to it.
Consider it dead.
See it crucified and buried with Christ.
Your new nature is at rest in me.

---

[1] Psalm 17:8; Proverbs 7:2; Deuteronomy 32:10; Zechariah 2:8.
[2] Zephaniah 3:17.
[3] Hebrews 4:1-11; Matthew 11:28-30.
[4] Romans 6:6; Romans 7:5 (NLT); Ephesians 4:22 (NLT); Colossians 3:9.

November 4

My treasure, my love:
I love this place where we are –
You and I, stuck.
Just stuck.
But together.
Together!
Think of it.
We are together.
We are living and breathing as one.[1]
It is so very beautiful, this togetherness.
There really is nothing more that is needed.
You don't need to do anything.
Just be with me.
Just enjoy my closeness.
Notice my tender caress in your body, soul and spirit.
And rest.
I've looked after everything for you.[2]
Rest, my love.[3]
In due time I will show you the next step.
For now, let's enjoy this being stuck.
Together.
Being stuck, together –
I like it!

---

[1] John 14:23; 1 Corinthians 3:16; 1 John 4:15; John 17:20-23; Revelation 3:20.
[2] Psalm 23; Psalm 116:7.
[3] Hebrews 4:9-11; Matthew 11:28-30.

November 5

My treasure, my love:
My love for you is enormous.[1]
It reaches from heaven to earth.
Nothing can separate you from my love.[2]
You are immersed in it.
It is carrying you along
in the current of my plan and purpose.
If you feel like you are floundering
and you are not sure of the way to go,
do not worry,
because I am carrying you.[3]
My love is carrying you
in the current of my will and my way.
So relax.
Let yourself be carried, swept along, by my love.
My love is everything because I **am** love.[4]
The cross of Christ is the greatest demonstration of my love.[5]

---

[1] Psalm 36:5; Psalm 103:11; Ephesians 3:17-19.
[2] Romans 8:38-39.
[3] Exodus 19:4; Deuteronomy 1:31; Deuteronomy 32:11.
[4] 1 John 4:16.
[5] Titus 3:4-6; 1 John 4:9-10.

November 6

Ah my treasure, my love:
Here we are in this sacred space once more -
This space where we commune,[1]
where we experience the wholeness and contentment
that derives from our oneness.
My treasure,
I have been closer than your heartbeat
through this entire experience.
I surely carried you[2]
when you were too weak
to even know where you were.
This water of adversity has not swept you away,[3]
but rather is being used to do a sorting and a sifting
that will bring positive change.
The truth is that nothing can separate you from my love,[4]
not physical pain or disorientation
or loss of physical or mental or emotional function.
When you cried out to me for help,
that cry was the breath of my Spirit within you,
interceding for you with groans too deep for words.[5]
I am answering those prayers, my love!

---

[1] John 14:23; 1 Corinthians 3:16; Ephesians 2:6; 1 John 4:16; Revelation 3:20.
[2] Exodus 19:4; Deuteronomy 1:31; Deuteronomy 32:11.
[3] Psalm 18:16; Psalm 32:6.
[4] Romans 8:38-39.
[5] Romans 8:26.

November 7

My treasure, my love:
You are the apple of my eye.[1]
It's preposterous to think that I am passing you by!
No, I am painstakingly preparing you
for the work I ordained for you
before I created the earth.[2]
And, in the meantime,
I am using you to build my Kingdom.[3]
My love, you are very precious to me.
I approve of you entirely![4]
It is not accurate to see yourself
standing on the periphery of my activity,
for you are in the midst of what I am doing.
It is not accurate to see yourself
waiting to be chosen,
for I have chosen you![5]
It is not accurate to see yourself
apart from me, waiting for me to come,
because I have come –
you and I are one already:
You in me, I in you,[6] doing the will of God.
So, all is well.
See yourself in the flow of God's activity,
in God's river of love,[7]
enjoying being buoyed up by the waves of the Spirit.

---

[1] Psalm 17:8; Proverbs 7:2; Deuteronomy 32:10; Zechariah 2:8.
[2] Psalm 139:16; Isaiah 37:26.
[3] Luke 9:2.
[4] Zephaniah 3:17.
[5] 1 Peter 2:9.
[6] John 14:23; 1 John 4:16; Revelation 3:20.
[7] Psalm 36:7-8;

November 8

My love, my treasure:
Still your soul[1] and listen to my voice.
If you could see the magnitude of my love for you,[2]
you would cast your worries aside!
Trust in my love for it knows no limits.[3]
Regarding your position:
You are where you are because I have placed you there.
I have given you your position and your role
and the power to function in it.
You are there as my representative and in my stead.
You stand in my authority and in my glory.[4]

---

[1] Psalm 131:2; Psalm 62:1.
[2] Psalm 36:5; Psalm 103:11 (NLT); Ephesians 3:17-19.
[3] Psalm 36:7 (NLT).
[4] Titus 2:15; 2 Timothy 1:7; 1 Peter 4:10-11; Ephesians 3:20.

November 9

My love:
I am guiding you,[1] protecting you,[2] and providing[3] for you
just as I did this for Jesus when he walked on the earth.
In fact, both Jesus and I are with you
through the indwelling presence of our Holy Spirit. [4]
We are at work in you,
causing you to will and to do our purpose.[5]
As you fix your thoughts on us and put your trust in us,
we will keep you in perfect peace.[6]

---

[1] Psalm 16:7 (NLT); Psalm 31:3.
[2] Psalm 41:2; Psalm 86:2 (NLT).
[3] Jeremiah 31:12; Philippians 4:19.
[4] 1 Corinthians 3:16; Romans 8:11.
[5] Philippians 2:13.
[6] Isaiah 26:3; Philippians 4:6-7.

November 10

My treasure, my love:

I love you![1]

Now is the time to be bold in your faith.[2]

Now is the time to ask me for what I have placed in your heart.

Now is the time to trust

that I will accomplish more than you can ask or imagine.[3]

Now is the time to spread your wings and fly.

Now is the time to forget the past

and to seize what I am doing today.

---

[1] John 17:20-23.
[2] 2 Corinthians 3:12.
[3] Ephesians 3:20.

November 11

Dearest friend:
Let me be your motivation.
Let me be your will.[1]
Let me be your everything.
My love is with you in all things –
including this challenge.[2]
Let me be the wind in your sails.
Let me be your sails.
Let me be your joy.[3]
Let me be your everything.
Let me be your peace.[4]
Let me be your strong defense.[5]
Let me be your comfort.[6]
Let me be everything you need.
Let me be your humility, your surrender, your obedience.
Let me be your life.[7]
Give me your independence
and let me replace it with my (Jesus')
dependence on God for every breath and every move.[8]
Give me your will
and I will give you mine.
See yourself immersed in me and me in you.[9]

---

[1] Philippians 2:13.
[2] Isaiah 43:2.
[3] Romans 14:17; Nehemiah 8:10.
[4] Romans 5:1; Ephesians 2:14.
[5] Psalm 27:1; Psalm 28:8.
[6] 2 Corinthians 1:4; Isaiah 66:13.
[7] Galatians 2:20.
[8] John 5:19; Philippians 2:8.
[9] John 15:9; John 17:26; 1 John 4:16.

November 12

My treasure, my love:
You are mine and I am yours.[1]
This is the truth on which to base your life.
This is your place of belonging.
This is your place to stand.

---

[1] Isaiah 43:1,3; Malachi 3:17; Ezekiel 34:31; Isaiah 41:10; Song of Solomon 6:3.

November 13

My precious child,
I am with you in the midst of your deliberations.[1]
I hear your questions.
I know your insecurities.
Be assured that I am with you.
I am working out my purpose in and through your life.[2]
All the days of your life are written in my book[3]
and I am motivating you to pray for what I have written.[4]
And what I have written, I have written!
It surely will come into being.[5]
So lift up your head
and run with what you have been given.
It is an expression of what is in my heart
and written in my book.
Let compassion be your guide (for that is my essence)[6]
and run with what you have been given.
Shake off all doubt and hesitance.
I will equip you and empower you to succeed.[7]
It is done.
From my perspective, my love,
it already has been accomplished.
You will pray it into being.
Your prayers are the foundation and framework of this work.
So pray, believing that I will accomplish
all that you can ask or imagine and more![8]

---

[1] Matthew 28:20b.
[2] Ephesians 1:11; Isaiah 46:10.
[3] Psalm 139:16.
[4] Philippians 2:13.
[5] Joshua 21:45; Isaiah 14:24.
[6] 1 John 4:16.
[7] Colossians 1:11; Philippians 4:13; Acts 1:8.
[8] Ephesians 3:20.

November 14

My treasure, my love:
You have crawled onto my throne,
you have taken my gavel,
and you are judging and condemning yourself quite harshly!
I recommend that you stop –
judgment is mine and mine alone.[1]
You simply are not equipped to judge,
particularly because you see in part,
you understand in part,
and you love in part.
Leave judging to me.

---

[1] James 4:12; Romans 14:4.

November 15

Precious friend:
Come to me and take my yoke.[1]
In order to take my yoke,
you will have to lay down everything you are carrying:
Your worries and concerns.
Your plans and dreams.
Your loves and interests.
Your expectations and illusions.
Your habits and traditions and ways of being.
All that you hold dear.
When you have divested yourself of everything,
then take up my yoke,
for "my yoke is easy and my burden is light."[2]
The reason my yoke is easy
is because you can't pick it up
until you have let go of all your attachments
to the things of earth,
and when you have let go of every attachment –
including being attached to life itself –
then you are free.
My yoke is characterized by being free
to live and move and be in me.[3]
My burden is light because God is carrying it.

---

[1] Matthew 11:29.
[2] Matthew 11:30 (NIV).
[3] Acts 17:28.

November 16

My child:
"Be still, and know that I am God."[1]
I am your God[2]
and I am intimately involved
in every detail of your life.[3]
In fact, it is in me
that you live and move and have your being.[4]
So, you and I are inseparable,
and I like it that way!
Do you know that the energy that is you, is I?[5]
That everything you do, you do with my energy, my life?
Whatever you are doing, you are doing with my life.
When what you are doing – including resting –
is in line with my will,
then it is accompanied by a sense of wellbeing.
When what you are doing is outside of my will,
then it is accompanied by a sense of unrest.
Doing my will always is accompanied by peace and joy,
even if it is painful or arduous.
When you ask me to tell you what I want you to do,
and my response is to ask you what you would like to do,
I am inviting you to imagine yourself doing all the possibilities. By
paying attention to the sense of peace or unrest
that accompanies each thing you imagine,
you can discover my will.

---

[1] Psalm 46:10a (ESV).
[2] Ezekiel 34:31.
[3] Psalm 139.
[4] Acts 17:28.
[5] Galatians 2:20.

November 17

My treasure, my love:
Today I want to talk to you about solace.
In this life you will experience
distress, disappointment, and tedium.
You can count on my Spirit to bring you comfort in those times.[1]
That is why Jesus got in a boat to be by himself
after he heard about John the Baptist's demise.
He was seeking solace.
Let me be your solace when you are
distressed, disappointed or experiencing tedium.

---

[1] 2 Corinthians 1:3; Isaiah 66:13.

November 18

Beautiful friend:
While you certainly have experienced a shipwreck,
you are not a wreck of a person!
In fact, this experience is serving the purpose
of major character development.[1]
You'll see.
To get there, all you need to do is to stay close to me.[2]
I am guiding you every step of the way.[3]
My treasure:
Lean heavily on me as you navigate this journey.[4]
It does not matter that you have not been this way before –
I know the way.
It does not matter that you cannot see what lies ahead –
I have been there.
It does not matter that you feel ill equipped for the journey –
I am providing everything you need all along the way.[5]
Beautiful friend:
Let my joy be your strength.[6]

---

[1] Romans 5:3-4.
[2] Joshua 22:5 (NLT); John 15:4.
[3] Psalm 32:8 (NLT).
[4] Isaiah 50:10 (NLT); Proverbs 3:5.
[5] Philippians 4:19.
[6] Nehemiah 8:10.

November 19

My treasure, my love:
"Do not let your heart be troubled...
Believe...in me."[1]
Believe in my goodness.[2]
Believe in my tender, loving care for you.[3]
Believe that I will deliver you from this dark place.[4]
Believe that I have provided for you –
past, present, and future.[5]
Do not look at the circumstances;
look at my loving faithfulness.[6]
Choose to believe, my love.
Let go of all your doubts and trust in me.
Put your hope in me because I am totally trustworthy.[7]
Focus on the things that give you joy and wait.
Wait to see how I deliver you.[8]
Wait to see how I lift you up to a high place.[9]

---

[1] John 14:1 (NASB).
[2] Psalm 145:9; 1 Peter 2:3.
[3] Psalm 69:16; Isaiah 63:7.
[4] Psalm 18:2; Ezekiel 34:12.
[5] Psalm 23:1; Philippians 4:19.
[6] Psalm 100:5.
[7] Hebrews 10:23.
[8] Psalm 27:14.
[9] James 4:10; 1 Peter 5:6.

November 20

My treasure, my love:

Bring all your concerns to me and convert them into requests.[1]

I am willing and more than able to answer all your prayers.[2]

It's not about figuring out how prayer works, my love.

It's about believing.

---

[1] Philippians 4:6.

[2] Psalm 55:22 (NLT); 2 Corinthians 9:8; 1 Peter 5:7; Ephesians 3:20.

November 21

My treasure, my love:
Rest.
Rest in me.[1]
Rest assured that I am looking after you.
Know that all your needs are met in me.[2]
I will make a way where there seems to be no way.[3]
I am in the business –
in fact, it is my specialty –
of changing my children's hearts.[4]
This includes yours.
So be at rest.
I am creating in you a heart of expectant faith.[5]
Watch and wait.[6]
And enter my rest.
I have done it all,
so you might as well enter into my joy right now![7]
You can be carefree and full of joy
because it is already accomplished in heaven
and will be done on earth.[8]
Be at peace,[9] my love,
because I am your God
and my love sustains you.
Rest in my love.
Rest.

[1] Matthew 11:28-29; Hebrews 4:9-10.
[2] Philippians 4:19.
[3] Isaiah 43:19.
[4] Ezekiel 36:26; Luke 1:17.
[5] Hebrews 10:22a (NLT).
[6] Micah 7:7.
[7] Matthew 25:21.
[8] Matthew 6:10.
[9] John 14:27.

November 22

My love, my treasure:
You can be 100% confident
in my love and my grace and my provision.[1]
As I have been telling you,
I already have provided all you need.[2]
You receive it by believing.[3]
Nothing will change this because I do not change.[4]
I love you with an everlasting love[5]
and nothing can separate you from my love.[6]
As you focus on my love and grace,
you will grow in your ability to trust me.
I'm looking after this development.
So relax.
Enjoy each day.
Live in a place of gratitude[7]
for the grace you have experienced,
the grace you are experiencing,
and the grace you will experience in the future.

---

[1] Romans 4:21.
[2] Psalm 23:1; 2 Corinthians 9:8; Philippians 4:19.
[3] Mark 11:24.
[4] Malachi 3:6a; James 1:17.
[5] Jeremiah 31:3.
[6] Romans 8:38-39.
[7] Colossians 2:6-7; Colossians 3:16; Hebrews 12:28.

November 23

My treasure, my love:
I am within you,[1] guiding your every step.[2]
I am planting within you my plans for your life.[3]
They are like seedlings that are taking root and growing.
In the fullness of time,
they will produce an abundant harvest
of good works in my Kingdom.
I am responsible for this from beginning to end.
Your task is to remain in me[4] –
to keep your face turned to me always.[5]

[1] 1 Corinthians 3:16; John 14:23; 1 John 4:16.
[2] Psalm 32:8 (NLT); Psalm 73:24; Isaiah 48:17.
[3] Psalm 138:8 (NLT); Jeremiah 29:11; Philippians 1:6.
[4] John 15:4.
[5] Psalm 27:8; Psalm 123:2; 1 Chronicles 16:11; Psalm 105:4; Hebrews 12:2.

November 24

My treasure, my love:
Let me hold you in my arms[1]
and kiss away your tears.
Let my strength
pour into your aching body, soul and spirit.
I am a God of justice[2]
and I will right this wrong.
Leave it with me[3]
and pursue your future with enthusiasm.

---

[1] Isaiah 46:4; Deuteronomy 1:31.
[2] Psalm 50:6 (NLT); Isaiah 30:18.
[3] Isaiah 51:5 (NLT).

November 25

My love:
It's great that you are exploring options that arise.
It is only through this exploration
that you discover whether something is what you want to do.
Remember that exploration does not obligate you to proceed
if you realize that something is not a good fit for you.
Draw close to me,[1] my love,
and sense your fears dissipate.
I am love and there is no fear in love.[2]
I am guiding you along the best path for your life[3]
so there is nothing to fear.
I did not bring you all this way to abandon you to your fears!
No, my best for you includes joy and love and laughter.
It includes fun and games, dinners and delights.
You have worked very hard in my vineyard
and it gives me joy to see you relax
and enjoy the pleasures in life.[4]
You will again put your hand to the plough.
There is a season for everything,[5] my love.

---

[1] James 4:8a; Hebrews 7:19 (NIV).
[2] 1 John 4:16-18.
[3] Psalm 32:8 (NIV).
[4] Psalm 37:27.
[5] Ecclesiastes 3:1 (NIV).

November 26

My treasure, my love:
Throw off constraints, lift up your head, and laugh.[1]
Laugh at adversity –
all it can do is make you stronger.
Laugh at temptation –
all it can do is grow your faith.
Laugh at negativity –
all it can do is increase your determination to experience joy.
So laugh, my love!
I am your God and I have everything in hand.[2]
When you look back on this time,
you will see my meticulous guidance.[3]
So you might as well enter into my rest now.[4]
It's all already accomplished.
Join me in resting and waiting
for my will to be revealed
in the fullness of time.

---

[1] Proverbs 31:25 (NIV).
[2] Hebrews 1:3a; Colossians 1:16-17.
[3] Psalm 138:8 (NIV).
[4] Hebrews 4:1-11; Matthew 11:28-30.

November 27

My treasure, my love:
There is a time to grieve.[1]
Honor this time.
Give yourself permission
to cry the tears and feel the sadness.
There is no point in trying to curtail it.
Eventually grief will give way to joy.[2]

---

[1] Ecclesiastes 3:4.
[2] Psalm 126:5.

November 28

My love, my treasure:
You are experiencing fear because you are looking
at your apparently impossible circumstance.
What you are forgetting
is that I deliberately set up humanly impossible circumstances.
They are designed to test and grow your faith.[1]
Nothing is impossible for me.[2]
Walk into the future with confidence,
knowing that I am your Lord.
Wait and watch in expectant hope and faith
to see what I have prepared for you.[3]
You are my treasure.
You are my love.
You are my child[4]
and I am pleased to establish you
in a place of fruitfulness.[5]

---

[1] James 1:2-4; Romans 5:3-4; 1 Peter 1:6-7.
[2] Mark 10:27; Jeremiah 32:17.
[3] Matthew 25:34; John 14:2; 1 Peter 1:3-4.
[4] John 1:12; Romans 8:16; Galatians 3:26; 1 John 3:1.
[5] John 15:1-8; Philippians 1:9-11.

November 29

My treasure, my love:
This is one of those times
when I am asking you to trust me
even though what is happening
does not make sense to you
and is not pleasing to you.
Will you do that?
What I am asking of you
is similar to what I asked of Abraham
when I moved him out of his home in Harran:[1]
to step out into the unknown, the unfamiliar, the uncomfortable.
You will need to trust
that I truly am causing you to will and to do my pleasure.[2]
Will you do that?
You also will need to trust
that I actually will "work out (my) plans for (your) life"[3]
and that I am "(guiding) you
along the best pathway for your life."[4]
Will you choose to trust me?
Will you choose to embrace what I am doing?

---

[1] Genesis 12:1-6.
[2] Philippians 2:13.
[3] Psalm 138:8a (NLT).
[4] Psalm 32:8a (NLT).

November 30

My treasure, my love:
When you imagine
that others are judging and condemning you,
they become gods to you.
This leads to bondage –
to a restricting of your freedom.
It restricts your freedom
to relax, to belong,
and to experience joy.
It restricts your freedom
to see what I am doing
and to see your part in my plans and purposes.
It impedes your ability
to confidently and joyfully proceed
with your mission in my Kingdom.
I alone am your God,[1] my love.
Be done with this idol worship so you can be free.

---

[1] Exodus 20:3; Luke 4:8.

December

December 1

My love, my treasure:
Each day we live and work together, you and I.[1]
Closer than hand in hand we move forward as one.
You have asked me for this
and I am fulfilling your request.
Even when you are not aware of it,
I am filling you with my Spirit[2]
and empowering you to do
what I have ordained for your life.[3]
You are right in thinking
that if I took you today to be with me,
nothing would be lost –
It is better by far to be with me in Paradise.[4]
However, my plan for you now
is to live and love and laugh in oneness with me on earth.
You are wondering
about where you will be working one year from now.
Well, I am not wondering! I know this detail.
I am going ahead of you
and arranging what is written in my book.[5]
When the time is right, it will become clear to you.
In the meantime, enjoy what I have provided for today.
You are wondering how you can believe for something
when you don't know what that something is.
When you don't know the exact nature of the thing,
you can believe in general
that I will provide exactly what is needed.

[1] Acts 17:28.
[2] Ephesians 5:18b.
[3] Ephesians 3:16; 2 Peter 1:3.
[4] Philippians 1:23; Luke 23:43.
[5] Deuteronomy 31:8; Psalm 139:16.

December 2

My love, my treasure:
"Be still, and know that I am God."[1]
Be still and listen to my soft and gentle voice
speaking in your spirit.[2]
My preference is to speak in whispers –
soft, gentle words that caress your spirit
like a breeze caresses your cheek.
It is best this way, because it requires that you be still.[3]
Do you know
that there is never a time when I am not there,
speaking to you in the silence?
Yes, and the words I speak
always are words of tender love.[4]
Always.
Always tender love.
Take time to be still every day
and to listen for this tender love.
It is your life.
It is the well from which you draw
all that you ever will need
in this life or the next.
My beautiful child,[5]
listen often for this Word of Love.

Sometimes, in addition to this Word of Love,

---

[1] Psalm 46:10a (ESV).
[2] 1 Kings 19:11-13.
[3] Psalm 131:2; Psalm 62:1.
[4] 1 John 4:16.
[5] 1 John 3:1.

I will have other things to share with you —
Words of Life that speak to certain situations.
Like today.
Today I want to talk to you
about what is happening in your life.
I want you to know
that I have heard all your prayers
and I am answering them.
These things you are experiencing —
the awkward and uncomfortable things —
these are evidence of my being at work,
answering your prayers.
You can resist what I am doing
and make it even more uncomfortable,
or you can choose to be accepting
and make it easier and less time-consuming.
Learn to say, "Yes, Lord, to your will and to your way"
at all times.
Let this response be your default response.
I will help you with this.[1]

And so, my love,
let me again reassure you of my love for you.
Yes, I will say it again and again!
My love for you is boundless![2]
You really are completely and totally immersed in my love.

---

[1] Philippians 2:13.
[2] Psalm 103:11 (NLT); Ephesians 3:17b-19.

December 3

My love, my treasure:
I love to talk to you!
You are my dearly beloved child.[1]
Today I invite you to come up here with me.
Come see your life from my perspective in the heavenlies.[2]
What seems at close view to be a meaningless jumble,
actually is a beautiful pattern when seen from up here.
I have planned a beautiful future for you,[3]
and now is not the time
for you to know the intricacies of that plan.
"Be still, and know that I am God."[4]
Be still, and know
that I have begun a good work in you
and I will be faithful to complete it.[5]
Be still, and know
that as you continue to "delight yourself in (me,
I) will give you the desires of your heart."[6]
Rest in me, my love. Rest.[7]

[1] John 1:12; 1 John 3:1.
[2] Ephesians 2:6.
[3] Jeremiah 29:11.
[4] Psalm 46:10a (ESV).
[5] Philippians 1:6.
[6] Psalm 37:4 (ESV).
[7] Matthew 11:28-29; Hebrews 4:9-10.

December 4

My love, my treasure:
Stand on the rock – Jesus Christ.[1]
Stand on his finished work of redemption.
This life on earth is such a tiny piece of eternity.
Live it in light of the finished work of Jesus Christ.[2]
Live it in the light of the victory already won.[3]
Live it in the light of the revelation of the Apostle John.[4]
All is well, my love.
All is well.

---

[1] Psalm 18:2; Psalm 40:2; Matthew 7:24; Ephesians 2:20.
[2] John 17:4; John 19:30; Colossians 1:13-14.
[3] 1 John 5:4.
[4] The last book in the New Testament, named "Revelation."

December 5

My treasure, my love:
Yes!
When you choose to accept what I am providing,
you are choosing life.[1]
When you choose to resist what I am providing,
you are choosing death.
You have just stepped over from death into life.
Are you sensing the relaxation in your body?
You are entering into my rest![2]
You can't embrace and enjoy what you have
if you are hankering for what you do not have.

---

[1] Deuteronomy 30:19-20.
[2] Matthew 11:28-29; Hebrews 4:9-10.

December 6

My treasure, my love:
This is most exquisite pain.
I know –
I'm feeling it together with you.[1]
Estrangement is accompanied by such anguish.[2]
Please remember that this situation is temporary.
And remember that I am at work.
Advent is about sitting in darkness
and waiting for that great light.[3]
That is your task:
to wait in this place where you can't see the light,
expecting me to come.
Expecting me to come with revelation.
I will wait with you.
Let me do your expecting for you.
Later on, when the light has dawned,
you will look back on this time of waiting
and smile regarding the intensity of your pain.
Your faith will be rewarded.[4]
You'll see.
So let's start being happy about that right now.
Why not?
It's better than being miserable, is it not?

---

[1] John 14:23.
[2] Psalm 55:4-8, 12-14.
[3] Matthew 4:16.
[4] Mark 10:51-52.

December 7

My treasure, my love:
Come.
Come to me.[1]
Rest in me.
Know that you are yoked with me.[2]
It doesn't really matter what is happening
because we are together.
We are in it together.
Whatever is happening,
we are experiencing it together.
Bring to your awareness
my presence with you and within you.

---

[1] Matthew 11:28.
[2] Matthew 11:29.

December 8

My treasure, my love:
Sometimes you come to me all apologetic
when there is nothing to forgive![1]
I'm actually just enjoying you and delighting in you.[2]
I don't set unreasonable and unrealistic standards for you,
my love.
I want you to enjoy your life[3]
and practice celebrating my presence
as you proceed.
All is well.
All is well.

---

[1] Romans 8:1.
[2] Zephaniah 3:17 (NLT).
[3] Psalm 35:27; Psalm 149:4.

December 9

My treasure, my love:
Be assured that I am working out my purpose.[1]
Am I not God Almighty?[2]
Look again to the One you serve.
Look at my might, my omniscience.
Look at the fact that I have predetermined the end.[3]
Look again at my tender loving care for you.[4]
My treasure, my love:
Events are unfolding according to my plan.[5]
Even the things that are painful
have a role to play in my plan.
Rest in me,[6] my love.
Rest and know that I am your doting parent
and I will meet all your needs.[7]
I already have met your needs –
the provision is on its way!
Lift up your head and be glad.
Lift you your head and laugh, my treasure.
Lift up your head and enjoy each day
as it unfolds according to my plan.
I am God.
I am **your** God.[8]
I AM.[9]

---

[1] Ephesians 1:11; Isaiah 46:10.
[2] Genesis 35:11; Genesis 17:1; Revelation 11:17.
[3] Revelation 1:1-3.
[4] Psalm 69:16; 1 Peter 5:7.
[5] Psalm 138:8 (NLT).
[6] Matthew 11:28-29.
[7] Philippians 4:19.
[8] Isaiah 41:10, 13; Ezekiel 34:31.
[9] Exodus 3:14.

December 10

My love, my treasure:
Whether others consider themselves to be superior –
Whether others consider themselves to be entitled –
What is that to you?
You are mine.[1]
Your life is in my life.[2]
Your destiny is in my plan to redeem the world.[3]
Let it go, my love!
Let it go and move on.
And get your hopes up!
Think again about what you long for
and put your faith in me.
I am the God of the impossible.[4]

---

[1] Isaiah 43:1.
[2] Galatians 2:20.
[3] Ephesians 1:3-14.
[4] Mark 10:27; Jeremiah 32:17.

December 11

My love, my treasure:
Surrender to me, my love.
Surrender to all that I am doing in your life.[1]
Rest assured that I have your best interests at heart.[2]
I truly am looking after every detail.[3]
Take all of your cares and concerns
and leave them with me.[4]
I am strong and powerful to deal with everything.[5]
I don't want you to be upset about anything.
I want you to be free to enjoy
the table I have set before you.[6]
It's a table laden with many good things.[7]
Convert all your cares into requests and rest.[8]

---

[1] Psalm 37:5; Proverbs 3:5.

[2] Jeremiah 29:11.

[3] Psalm 138:8 (NLT).

[4] Philippians 4:6; 1 Peter 5:7.

[5] Deuteronomy 3:24; Exodus 15:11.

[6] Psalm 23:5a.

[7] James 1:17.

[8] Philippians 4:6-7.

December 12

My treasure, my love:
<u>You have nothing to fear</u>
because <u>I always am with you.</u>[1]
Yes, bad things happen,
but I am at work in the midst of everything.[2]
<u>Do not be afraid</u>.
I am protecting you in the midst of the bad things.
That's what is meant by the passage in Isaiah:
"...**When** you walk through the waters...
When you pass through the flames..."[3]
My promise is to be with you as you experience adversity.

---

[1] Matthew 28:20b.
[2] Genesis 50:20; Romans 8:28.
[3] Isaiah 43:2 (NASB, emphasis added).

December 13

"Be still, and know that I am God."[1]

All these things you consternate about –

"Be still, and know that I am God."[2]

I am leading you.[3]

I am guiding you.[4]

I am going on ahead of you

and preparing the way.[5]

You are walking in the path I have planned for you[6] so

"Be still, and know that I am God."[7]

You are my treasure, my love, my dearly beloved child[8]

and I am tenderly, patiently, persistently taking you by hand[9]

and walking with you through every experience

that I have ordained for you[10]

until finally I help you take the step over the threshold

from this life into the next[11] so

"Be still, and know that I am God."[12]

---

[1] Psalm 46:10a (ESV).
[2] Psalm 46:10a (ESV).
[3] Isaiah 48:17; Psalm 32:8 (NLT).
[4] Psalm 73:24; Isaiah 58:11; John 16:13.
[5] Deuteronomy 31:8; Ephesians 1:11; Psalm 37:23.
[6] Psalm 119:35.
[7] Psalm 46:10a (ESV).
[8] 1 Samuel 25:29 (NIV); Zephaniah 3:17; 1 John 3:1.
[9] Isaiah 42:6; Isaiah 41:13.
[10] Psalm 139:16.
[11] Psalm 73:24; John 14:3 (NLT).
[12] Psalm 46:10a (ESV).

December 14

My child, my love:
I am with you in the midst of this storm.[1]
My strong arms are surrounding you
and holding you up.[2]
You are not alone.
Lean on me[3]
and expect me to see you through to a better place.
I will redeem this
and use it to bring glory to my name.[4]
So do not be afraid.
Take heart and be encouraged.
Enter into my rest[5] –
I already have accomplished this for you.

---

[1] Isaiah 43:2; Matthew 28:20b.
[2] Isaiah 59:1 (NLT); Psalm 118:14-16 (NLT).
[3] Isaiah 50:10 (NLT); Proverbs 3:5.
[4] John 9:3; John 11:4.
[5] Hebrews 4:1-11; Matthew 11:28-30.

December 15

My love, my treasure:
You are wise to come to me with this care.[1]
I am providing this opportunity
for you to be stretched
in your ability to trust me.[2]
Remember that I am God.
I am your God
and you are in the palm of my hand.[3]
You have done nothing wrong
and even if you had,
I would fix it for you.
So do not worry.
I am with you.[4]
You are perfectly safe.
You are my chosen,[5] my beloved,[6]
and I am lifting you up.[7]
I am causing you to will and to do my purpose;[8]
leave the details to me.
Yes, leave the details to me.
I am in control.[9]
Lean on me.[10] Stand secure in me.
Enter into my rest[11] and experience my joy.[12]

---

[1] Psalm 55:22; 1 Peter 5:7.
[2] Romans 5:3-5; James 1:2-4.
[3] Isaiah 49:2; Isaiah 51:16; Isaiah 62:3.
[4] Matthew 28:20b.
[5] Ephesians 1:4; 1 Peter 2:9
[6] Song of Solomon 2:16; Song of Solomon 6:3.
[7] Psalm 3:3.
[8] Philippians 2:13.
[9] John 3:35.
[10] Isaiah 50:10; Proverbs 3:5.
[11] Hebrews 4:1-11; Matthew 11:28-30.
[12] Psalm 43:4 (NLT); Matthew 25:21.

December 16

My treasure, my love:
Still and quiet your soul.[1]
Fill your mind and heart
with the scenes you want to experience.
This is the act of believing
that you have received what you have requested.[2]
I heard the prayer you prayed
as you knelt beside your bed this evening.
You have nothing to fear –
Am I not your God?[3]
Am I not the God of the impossible?[4]
Turn your eyes to my power and grace.[5]
Turn your eyes to my loving kindness.[6]
All is well, my love.
All is well.

---

[1] Psalm 131:2; Psalm 62:1.
[2] Mark 11:24.
[3] Ezekiel 34:31; Isaiah 41:10.
[4] Mark 10:27; Jeremiah 32:17.
[5] Titus 2:11; 2 Corinthians 12:9; Acts 14:3 (NLT).
[6] Jeremiah 31:3; Psalm 36:7; Titus 3:4-5.

December 17

My treasure, my love:
What a journey we're on!
In this life, you have an opportunity to believe in me.
You have believed in me[1]
and there has been much great fruit –
Much great fruit!
Get serious about believing.
I have so much I want to give you and to do in and through you.
There is no limit to what you and I can do when you believe![2]
Figure out what you want, ask me for it, and believe![3]

---

[1] John 12:44; John 14:1.
[2] Ephesians 3:20; 2 Corinthians 9:8.
[3] Mark 11:24.

December 18

My treasure, my love:
Choose joy.[1]
Choose life[2] - Choose joy!
Simply choose joy.
It is your inheritance.[3]
It is your birthright.
Refuse to be miserable.

---

[1] John 15:9-12; John 16:24; John 17:13 (NLT).
[2] Deuteronomy 30:19.
[3] Isaiah 61:7; Psalm 16:11; Psalm 33:12 (NLT); Romans 14:17.

December 19

What is happening now is part of my plan.
I am the master potter.[1]
I have taken you back to my potter's wheel
where I am reshaping your life.
This is a painful process
that involves a time of being in transition.
It is a metamorphosis.
You cannot control this or even understand it.
So just let it go.
Leave this reshaping in my hands.

---

[1] Jeremiah 18:1-6.

December 20

My treasure, my love:
Yes—let go of all negativity.
As soon as you have expressed your pain, let it go.
I already have carried that pain and paid the price for it.[1]
So let it go.
Move into your heritage of joy.[2]

---

[1] Isaiah 53:4.
[2] Isaiah 61:7; Psalm 16:11; Psalm 33:12 (NLT); Romans 14:17.

December 21

My love, my treasure:
Come. Sit with me.
Still and quiet your soul in my presence.[1]
Breathe deeply of my love and care for you.[2]
Do not let your heart be troubled.
Believe in me.[3]
We are forging new pathways in your brain –
pathways that are imbued
with my loving presence and care for you.

---

[1] Psalm 131:2; Psalm 62:1.
[2] Psalm 31:7 (NLT); John 10:14-15.
[3] John 14:1.

December 22

My treasure, my love:
You are tackling the challenge
of picking up the pieces of your life
after this monstrous medical miasma.
Remember that nothing of importance has changed.
I am still your life[1] and your life still is hidden in me.[2]
You and I will continue to walk together on this earth
until it is time for you to join me
in the place I have prepared for you.[3]
Simply enjoy what each day has to offer
as you do what I motivate you to do.[4]
Take time to sense the warm embrace of my love.[5]

[1] Galatians 2:20.
[2] Colossians 3:3.
[3] John 14:3.
[4] Philippians 2:13.
[5] Zephaniah 3:17 (NLT).

December 23

My treasure, my love:
The celebration of the birth of my Son begins tomorrow.
What a birthday that was!
Divinity in the form of a vulnerable infant!
I want you to know that I was perfectly calm about his wellbeing.
I had all the details of his life in hand.[1]
He faced many dangers and obstacles
but nothing took me by surprise.
I had prepared for all these eventualities.
My specialty is to bring good out of that which is negative.[2]
Sometimes the bad is necessary for the good to appear.
The primary example of this is the death of my Son.
That was truly bad,
and I brought the very best out of it.[3]
I'm doing the same in your life.
You have experienced some adversity –
some things that are truly bad.
I am at work in all of those things,
bringing good for you.
In time you'll see.
In the meantime,
surrender all these things to me.
Wait in expectant hope[4]
for the unfolding of my best for you.[5]

---

[1] John 12:16.
[2] Romans 8:28.
[3] Colossians 1:19-22
[4] Romans 8:25.
[5] Jeremiah 29:11.

December 24

My love, my treasure:
Lift up your heart and be glad.
Do you know why I am saying this?
I am saying this
because you have so much for which to be glad:
Your name is written in my Book of Life.[1]
I have given you the gift of eternal life.[2]
I am living within you.[3]
I am giving you a hope and a future.[4]
I am your doting heavenly parent.[5]
I love you passionately – just as you are.[6]
I am looking after all the details of your life.[7]
I am causing everything to work together for your good.[8]
I am your beloved and you are mine.[9]
I am creating beauty out of your ashes
and replacing your despair with praise.[10]
So lift up your head and be very glad,
My treasure, my love!

---

[1] Luke 10:20; Philippians 4:3; Revelation 3:5.
[2] Romans 6:23.
[3] Galatians 2:20.
[4] Jeremiah 29:11.
[5] 1 John 3:1; Galatians 3:26.
[6] Zephaniah 3:17.
[7] Psalm 138:8 (NLT).
[8] Romans 8:28.
[9] Song of Solomon 2:16; Song of Solomon 6:3.
[10] Isaiah 61:3.

December 25

Still and quiet your soul,[1] my love,
and listen to my still small voice.[2]
I am within you making everything new.[3]
I am transforming
your mind, your body, your heart, and your will.
You can cooperate with this process
by surrendering to me each day.[4]
Your act of surrender clears the way
for me to do this transforming work.
Surrendering is not just something you do
when you are experiencing fear.
No, my desire is for you to live a life of surrender.
Take your cue from Jesus
and surrender to me minute by minute.[5]
You will find that the surrendered life is a life of power.
The surrendered life is a life of love.
The surrendered life is a life of service.
The surrendered life is a life of peace and joy.
The surrendered life is a life of victory.
I have chosen to live in you[6]
and to hide your life in me[7]
so that you can live a surrendered life.
That, my love, is the Good News that Jesus came to bring.[8]
Enjoy Christmas this year, celebrating this Good News.

---

[1] Psalm 131:2; Psalm 62:1.
[2] 1 Kings 19:11-13.
[3] Romans 12:2 (NLT); 2 Corinthians 3:18 (NLT); 1 Corinthians 15:51-54.
[4] Psalm 37:5; Proverbs 3:5; Matthew 6:10.
[5] Philippians 2:5-11; Luke 22:42.
[6] 1 Corinthians 3:16; John 14:23; 1 John 4:16.
[7] Colossians 3:3.
[8] Luke 2:10-11.

December 26

My joy and delight:
Sometimes you are not able to release things into my care.
This is because you do not yet know
the full extent of my love.[1]
You do not know
that nothing can separate you from my love.[2]
You do not know
that you are in my love[3]
and you are safe in my love.[4]
You have experienced the conditional nature of human love.
My love for you, however, is not conditional and it is enough.[5]
It is all you need.
It is more than enough!
My love surrounds you and fills you.
My love supports you and heals you.
My love keeps you safe and energizes you.
My love is all you need.
Let me hold you in my love.
Let me carry you in my love.
Let me keep you safe in my love.
Celebrate my love; cherish my love.
Imagine yourself swimming in my love.
Imagine yourself buoyed up by my love
and warmed by my love,
My joy and my delight.

---

[1] Ephesians 3:16-19; Psalm 103:11 (NLT).
[2] Romans 8:38-39.
[3] Colossians 3:3.
[4] 1 John 4:18; Jude 1:21 (NLT).
[5] Romans 5:8; Psalm 103:11 (NLT).

December 27

I am cleansing you and shaping you
to be a vessel I can use.[1]
Do not resist this purifying process,
even though it is painful.[2]
I am the master silversmith[3]
and I will purify you until all that is seen
is my reflection shining in and through you.[4]

---

[1] Jeremiah 18:1-6.
[2] Romans 5:3-5; James 1:2-4; 1 Peter 4:12-13.
[3] Malachi 3:3.
[4] 2 Corinthians 3:18.

December 28

My love, my treasure:
As you live your life in simplicity and humility before me,
you will be able to enjoy inner peace and joy.[1]
Do what I give you the incentive and the grace to do[2]
and let go of anything else.
I love you,[3]
My treasure, my love!

---

[1] Romans 15:13.
[2] Philippians 2:13.
[3] Jeremiah 31:3; 1 John 4:16; 1 John 4:19.

December 29

You have asked me about what I am doing these days,
about how my Spirit is drawing my children close to me.[1]
My favorite way is through relationships.
Relationships are sacred.
All relationships are sacred.
Where people are interacting with each other,
I am there in my creating power.
Regard each interaction as a sacred opportunity
to work together with my Spirit
to draw people close to me.
You are yoked together with me in this endeavor.[2]
There is no need to sweat it – my yoke is easy.[3]
Just celebrate your connection with me
and then do and say what seems good at the time.

---

[1] John 6:44.
[2] Matthew 11:29.
[3] Matthew 11:30.

December 30

Precious friend:
I am here with you[1] in the stillness of this morning hour.
Do you notice what happens in your body
when you focus on my presence?
Yes, you experience peace.
You breathe more deeply,
the corners of your mouth begin to curve into a smile,
and all your muscles relax.
How lovely!
Let's just enjoy being together,
beautiful friend.

---

[1] Matthew 28:20b.

December 31

Beautiful treasure:
Yes, you truly have come to appreciate me.
Actually, the word "appreciate"
is quite inadequate to describe
how you regard me.
Truth be told, you have come
to adore, to adulate, and to treasure me.
You have come to know that I am your all in all.[1]
And that, my love, is what inspires your passion.
You have discovered the pearl of great price[2]
and you are determined to share this good news.
All your shattered dreams and dashed hopes
have not detracted from this primary mission in any way.
They are background noise and inconsequential,
except for how they have factored into the development
of your relationship with me.
That deep love you have for me?
It's a dim reflection of my immense love for you.[3]
You and I live and move in that love we share for each other.[4]
Even when you are not aware of it,
this is the context of your life.
Allow yourself to experience the deep peace
that comes from knowing these two things:
that you have found the most precious treasure of all
and that you are firmly established in your life purpose.

---

[1] 1 Corinthians 15:28.
[2] Matthew 13:45-46.
[3] Psalm 103:11 (NIV).
[4] Acts 17:28.

Subject Index

C

I

M

N

Acknowledgements

I would like, first, to thank my husband. Ken, it was you who eagerly listened when I wanted to share something that I sensed God say. It was you who began encouraging me years ago to put these communications into a book so others also could benefit from them. It was you who helped me conquer the doubt that has assailed me from time to time. Thank you, Ken, for your unflagging faith in me that has made this book possible.

I wonder if this book would still be waiting to be written were it not for my very dear friend and former colleague, Dr. Cheryl Noble. Thank you, Cheryl, for adamantly insisting that I must get these words out there, and now!

I also want to thank my precious friend, Amy Kuepfer, who beautifully provided emotional and spiritual support through the entire process. Thank you especially, Amy, for your insightful questions that have helped me find my way.

Four years ago, when I began planning a move from Ontario to Cranbrook, British Columbia, I began asking God for friends in my new home. Myfy, Marjorie, Karen, Marie, and Marilyn, you have been my mainstay during the entire time when I was putting together this book. Your friendship has kept me sane and grounded – thank you!

I am deeply grateful to those of you who took time out of your busy schedules to read what I have written and to write endorsements: Dr. Yme Woensdregt, Dr. Cheryl Noble, and Dr. Hazel Hill. Your words of affirmation are invaluable.

The support I have received from the publishing experts at Mission Publishing has been inestimable. Thank you especially to my gifted and wonderfully encouraging launch mentor, Viki Winterton.

It's possible that this book would not exist were it not for the wisdom that I received decades ago from my college music professors, Dr. George and Esther Wiebe. Thank you, George and Esther, for encouraging me to pray for the Spirit of God to fill my life at a critical time when I was doubting the existence of God.

I would like to thank Irene Pauls. It was in response to your suggestion that I began listening regularly to hear what God wants to say to me.

And finally, I want to thank God. Seriously, how do you manage to keep me faithfully drawing close to you and trying to hear what you are saying? It's a mystery and a miracle! I am so very grateful because my relationship with you is more precious to me than life.

About the Author,
Gwen Wellington

Gwen Wellington grew up on a farm in the foothills of southern Alberta. After graduating from High School, she studied music and theology for four years in Winnipeg, Manitoba at Canadian Mennonite Bible College (now Canadian Mennonite University).

Following graduation, she worked for the Conference of Mennonites in Canada, establishing a Christian Education Resource Centre for the churches across Canada. She also spent four years on Cape Croker Indian Reserve in Ontario, doing development work under Mennonite Central Committee together with her husband, Ken. Gwen then worked for several years with a lay ministry team, pastoring her home church. After earning a graduate degree in clinical social work, Gwen worked as a psychotherapist in the private practices she established first in Lethbridge, Alberta, and then in Markham, Ontario. While in Ontario, she and her husband served the Wideman Mennonite Church where Ken was the pastor for almost nine years. After twenty-four years of providing psychosocial counseling services, eventually specializing in psychological trauma, Gwen retired to Cranbrook, British Columbia.

Gwen summarizes her life's work as doing whatever she can to enable others to enhance the quality of their lives. She enjoys socializing with friends and family, making music, writing, sharing the word of God, creating lectin-free meals, and playing online Scrabble games with her husband. Gwen is the proud mother and grandmother of two children, their partners, and four grandchildren.

For more inspiration and motivation, visit Gwen's blog at www.wellington-author.com/blog/.

You also can connect with the author at www.wellington-author.com or www.facebook.com/GwenWellingtonAuthor.

Made in the USA
Coppell, TX
12 August 2020